WEAR MORE SILK

WEAR MORE SILK

131 luxurious
ways to add
romance, spice,
and adventure
to your
everyday life

BY JENNIFER "GIN" SANDER

FAIR WINDS
PRESS
GLOUCESTER, MASSACHUSETTS

A Big City Books Idea

Text © 2007 by Jennifer "Gin" Sander

First published in the USA in 2007 by
Fair Winds Press, a member of
Quayside Publishing Group
33 Commercial Street
Gloucester, MA 01930

11 10 09 08 07   1 2 3 4 5

ISBN - 13: 978-1-59233-194-9
ISBN -10: 1-59233-194-7

Library of Congress Cataloging-in-Publication
Data available

Cover and book design by
Laura McFadden Design, Inc.

Printed and bound in China

Magic doesn't come to those who don't expect it.

—DIANA VREELAND

Introduction

IT is often said that writers write the books they need. Let me tell you—without blushing—that is *indeed* the reason behind *Wear More Silk*. I recently began to notice that my life had become a tad too focused on the ordinary, and my relationship with my husband had grown a tad too focused on who wrote what check when. Sound familiar? It wasn't always like this, of course. Not only was my life as a single woman quite action-packed and adventurous, but so were my earliest years of marriage. But as the days and months pile up and the children arrive, who doesn't develop a tendency to sit around the house and watch life unfold on a television screen?

To spice things up, I began making little notes and drawing up lists of romantic, exciting, or just flat-out spicy things to do; sensual things to shake up our night life, so to speak; wild things to take us to new places; adventurous undertakings that would give us both something new to do and talk about (beyond our recent checking account activity).

I was reminded of a relationship book by Bobbie Sandoz-Merrill and Tom Merrill called *Settle for More*. The married coauthors encourage their readers to decide what kind of relationship they want and then act on it—moment to moment. For example, if you want a relationship of open communication, you have to tell him about the whopping credit card bill that just came in the mail. I realized that the exact same advice applies to how we live our whole lives: If it is a romantic and adventurous life we seek, the best way to achieve it is to fill the moments of our life with romantic and adventurous acts.

Our generation is notorious for being unsatisfied with what we have and always looking toward the future for something better. We have to learn how to focus our attention on the moment; to seize each little thrill and string them together like glowing pearls, making the strand longer and longer until we have built the life we truly desire.

I was languishing at work one morning, years ago, when the phone rang. It was a dashing friend who'd come up to northern California on a wine-buying trip. Could I meet him that afternoon for a private lunch at a winery? Heart pounding, I asked my boss for the rest of the day off. No problem, was the too-good-to-be-true reply, and a few moments later I was on my way out the door.

As I drove toward Napa, my favorite music blaring on the radio, dressed sharply in white linen, I thought to myself—*Yes!* This is the sort of life I want to have—rushing off for a gourmet adventure at the drop of a hat! And then suddenly it dawned on me. . .this *is* my life. If it weren't, I'd still be sitting at my desk working on a manuscript.

For me, romance is a mood, an image, a feeling that gives life a layer of mystery and magic. It doesn't necessarily have to lead to sex, though that's a lovely bonus. It can be adopting a hobby that takes you back to a simpler age, like English riding. It can be a sweet gesture like framing a beloved poem to hang above your fireplace.

Whatever your idea of romance is, it will change over the years. What is wildly romantic in your twenties is frighteningly bold in your forties. Be flexible. Look for the possibilities in small gestures. Wondrous things can come from something as simple as cooking with truffles (which were banned by the Victorians because they were believed to be too stimulating) or signing up for French lessons on the off chance that you might take a trip to Paris someday—anything that adds an extra kick or makes your life more vivid.

Your idea of adventure will also change. Remember that the more adventurous you and your partner are in life, the more adventuresome you are likely to be behind closed doors!

As you wander through the 131 ideas that follow, do keep something in mind: Men and women are very different, and so are their ideas about romance. My husband Peter's definition of romance is "something that happens spontaneously, not something staged and showy." So I won't ever be sending a flower-filled limo to pick him up before an event, and I guess I shouldn't expect to see him declare his love on the electronic scoreboard at an NBA basketball game.

One thing men and women would agree on: There is nothing romantic about going into debt or dealing with ongoing debt. Understand this—I don't want you to *buy* a new lifestyle; I want you to authentically create it with your imagination, creativity, and cunning. Yes, someday you might buy something adventurously expensive, but you will be genuinely knowledgeable and appreciative of this large purchase because you have been honing your romantic feelers in anticipation. I've tried to include plenty of ideas and suggestions that are either flat-out free or downright cheap.

It made a rather large impression on me years ago when a long-married man looked at me, sighed, and said, "You would never grow stale, would you?" Hmmm, no, I won't, and I filed that one in my brain under "how to keep your husband happy."

I hope there are ideas here that will inspire you to "freshen things up a bit"; ideas that will trigger you to take action; ideas that will make you reach for the phone book and make plans for tonight! Remember, it is up to you to be a full participant in life—don't sit around waiting for something to happen to you. Don't grow stale. Take matters into your own very capable hands and create the life of romance, adventure, and spice that you long for!

JENNIFER "GIN" SANDER
GRANITE BAY, CALIFORNIA

Backyard Oasis

~~~~~~

Wouldn't it be great if you and your loved one had a special, romantic rendezvous spot? Wouldn't it be amazing if that spot were conveniently located in your own backyard? If you build it, romance will come. Create a backyard sanctuary where you and your loved one can hide from the rest of the world and enjoy a quiet moment after dinner, or before anyone else in the house wakes up.

One option is a tent—not a heavy canvas tent that makes one think of bug bites and stale granola; but a few well-placed poles, some lightweight netting cast gently over them, a pile of silk cushions to lounge upon, and maybe a soft glowing lantern or a circle of candles surrounding you. Prefer to keep it simple? Hang a hammock in your backyard for after-dinner or lazy Sunday afternoon cuddling. Or find two extremely comfortable chairs and place them in the prettiest location in your yard. There you can sit—gazing out over your garden or staring into the evening sky—and sigh in unison. Once you have your backyard oasis set up, come up with as many excuses as you can to escape to it.

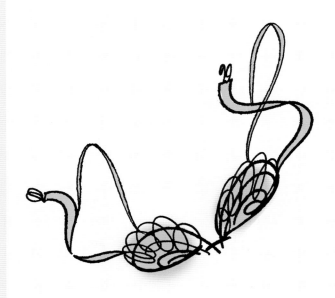

Lusty Tales

I once wrote a short novel called *Cigars: An Erotic Obsession* that I sent along with my husband on business trips a few pages at a time. Did it keep me in his thoughts? You bet it did. Try writing your own personal erotica. Buy yourself a fancy blank journal, sit down, and let your imagination go. . . describe your last sexual encounter, and then go back and embellish it. Was it at home in your own plain bed? Give yourself a sumptuous and expensive bed in which you and your love sank into the luxurious sheets. Use as much graphic description as you are in the mood for! Go ahead; no one is looking. . . . Although, wouldn't it be a bit of a spicy thrill to write your erotica in a busy café? There you'd be, happily jotting down juicy scenarios while all around you no one would suspect that the writing project you're so absorbed in is one that would make them blush.

Will you ever show this writing to anyone? It is entirely up to you. Keep it as a secret, or share it with your partner—you'll be surprised how effective a bit of personalized erotica can be as a seduction tool.

Snuggle for Warmth

Few textures are as warm and sensuous as real fur. Not only does it feel luxurious, but it also sends me back to a time when fur really was needed to keep warm at night. I sink into a fur pillow, close my eyes, and imagine the bare walls of a castle around me, the sound of leather boots walking down the wide hallway toward my chambers. . .don't I sound like the writer of a bodice-ripper?

Why toss out old furs when you can give them a place of pride in your home and maybe even a role in your love life? If you don't have any furs of your own, ask around in your family, and chances are someone has one to share. Whenever I come across vintage furs at garage sales, consignment shops, flea markets, or thrift stores, I snatch them up. I've had old fur coats fashioned into pillows, lap blankets to keep us warm and cozy next to a fire, and small bolsters to adorn our bed. For less than a hundred dollars, you could have a unique and cozy addition to your life. So snuggle up with someone on a fur rug by a flickering fire, close your eyes, and imagine you're escaping into the only source of warmth in a dark, remote castle....

Be Childlike Together

There is great romance and fun in loosening up and doing child-like things together, particularly if you do them *without* your children! So go ahead, write your initials or a love message in the sand; put a sappy poem in a bottle and toss it out to sea. Sit down together at an ice-cream store in the midst of a grown-up, busy day and order a big, messy banana split to share.

Don't forget to take this idea with you on your next romantic journey. My husband and I once stayed at a Ritz-Carlton in Half Moon Bay, where you can sit outside under the foggy night sky and roast marshmallows. We spent the entire evening giggling like a pair of kids, trying to brown the gooey marshmallows. For your next trip, pack some kiddie bubble bath in your suitcase or bring paper and crayons to pass the time on the plane flight. Bring junk food snacks to indulge in (a big box of Cap'n Crunch is divine!), or any little thing that makes you feel young and carefree. Consider renting bikes as a way of reconnecting with your childlike approach to life. Can you still show off and ride with no hands? Then throw them up in the air and celebrate your life of bold adventure with wild abandon!

Pleasant Surprise

Go shopping with your true love, and remember what it's like to think only of each other. Here's how it works: Pick a store that has something for you both: a big bookstore, a clothing store, a video store, or if you really want to be adventurous, an upscale sex shop. Split up to hunt for a secret gift for your partner, and agree to meet at an arranged time and location.

This is bound to turn into a sexy, grown-up game of peek-a-boo played out in public. You are shopping for him (and spying on him at the same time); he is shopping for you (and spying on you at the same time, too). While you are enjoying thinking of him and his needs, you can also enjoy the idea that he is close by, thinking of *your* needs.

Try to get through the check-out line without letting each other see what you've chosen, and then meet up in a cozy café for the gift exchange. Or you might want to keep your gifts in their anonymous paper bags until you get home for a more private gift exchange ceremony (particularly if you were playing this game in a sexy shop!).

You Smell Like... You

Adventurous women don't dress like everyone, they don't visit the same places as everyone, and they certainly don't smell like everyone! While custom-blended perfumes can cost thousands of dollars, here is a more affordable way to create a signature scent of your own.

Step one: Buy a small bottle of cheap vodka. It makes a great base for a scented body splash. Step two: Visit a health food store or beauty supply store that carries essential oils and choose a few that appeal to you.

Once you've got your ingredients, fill three quarters of a shot glass with vodka. Now begin your experiments to create the smell that best displays your personality. Are you a romantic dreamer? Try for a blend with flowery tones. A bold woman who speaks your mind? Blend together a spicy and woodsy scent that conveys your personal strength. Involve your partner in helping you create a scent that he likes, too. Some studies claim that cinnamon and vanilla are the scents that men find most appealing, so be sure to add at least a dash of vanilla to your mixture!

Sweet and Dry

Instead of "Life is too short to drink cheap champagne," my motto is, "Pay plenty for Prosecco." Whereas twenty-dollar champagne tastes like twenty-dollar champagne, spending twenty dollars on Prosecco, a lightly bubbled aperitif, brings extraordinary, unexpected delight. This explains why Italians drink it with just about every kind of meal.

In *A Thousand Days in Venice*, Marlena de Blasi describes a night out with her lover and the uniquely sensual appeal of Prosecco:

> *It's a Saturday evening and, with no aim, we float. Out on the deck of a vaporetto I pull Prosecco from my purse; the wine, having rested for an hour or so in the freezer, is achingly cold, its tight sharp bubbles an anesthetic on the tongue. He is timid, hoping no one will mistake him for a tourist, but he takes long hard pulls of the wine. 'Hai sempre avuto una borsa cosi ben fornita? Have you always had such a well-stocked purse?' he asks.*

Every glass of Prosecco gives you an opportunity to change an ordinary meal into one that conjures up the romance of Italy. So place a bottle of well-chilled Prosecco in your big purse before your next romantic outing and see where it takes you. All the way to Venice, perhaps!

Champagne Fantasies

I know I've been pushing you toward the Italian bubbly and away from the French, but I only mean to keep you away from disappointment. Once you do spring for a bottle of champagne or get one as a gift, what happens if you can't drink the whole thing? We all have to pour a bit of old red wine down the sink on occasion; but your heart will surely ache if you have to do the same with leftover champagne. What to do? Here are a few ideas to try out in the days after a big celebration.

- Add a splash of champagne to your bath. It won't actually do anything for your skin, but it will make you feel luxuriously decadent and sexy.
- Put it in your salad. Add leftover champagne to your regular oil and vinegar mixture for a bit of tang, but add it sparingly to avoid making your dressing too runny.
- Poach fish with leftover champagne. This works well for salmon and lobster as well.

Artistic Inspiration

Museums don't have to be stuffy and boring, especially when they're bursting with erotic art! The Museum of Sex in New York City, for example, and the Erotic Art Museums of Europe are filled with titillating sculptures, drawings, and paintings to enjoy arm in arm with a loved one. But you don't have to hop on a plane to enjoy erotic art.

Grab your guy, head to the closest city, and spend a day cruising museums looking for images that get you in the mood. Pay particular attention to the works of European painters like Courbet, whose *The Sleepers* and *The Origin of the World* were once banned from public display; Picasso, whose voyeuristic sketches and suggestive abstracts get the imagination flowing; and Degas, who painted women in seemingly private moments—bathing or combing their hair. Cruise the hall of Japanese art and maybe you'll find a shockingly explicit shunga, erotic art printed on wood blocks and scrolls. When you've had your fill, stop by the gift shop for a framed memento to hang in your bedroom. By the time you get home, you'll be eager to celebrate your worldliness by bringing your favorite erotic artwork to life!

Snowy Picnics

Tromping quietly through the snow on a mild, late winter afternoon with your true love, you hear only the sound of your shoes breaking through the crust and the gentle thud of old snow dropping from a nearby tree branch. You have the world to yourselves, a sparkling wonderland of white and blue and green. And you have a picnic in your backpack, of course.

Want to make an afternoon with your loved one more memorable? Cross-country ski, snowshoe, or hike into a snowy forest together. Plan carefully, well in advance, and wait for the weather to cooperate. Tuck a few carefully chosen items into your backpack, like a small bottle of wine (I pour mine into an empty water bottle to save the weight), cold chicken, and some chewy homemade brownies.

How do you sit and picnic in the snow? Find a big stump or rock, or use a waterproof blanket to keep your bottoms dry. Who knows what might happen out there in the wilderness with no one else around?

Change Your Hair

Many of us tend to stick to a look we feel comfortable with, and sometimes we stick to that look for waaay too long: same weight, same wardrobe, and same hairdo. Changing your weight overnight is tough without costly surgery, and changing your wardrobe is too great of a financial commitment, so why not temporarily change your hair? For one short day style it completely differently: part it on the other side, blow dry it straight, leave it naturally wavy—whatever goes against your normal rules. Go out in public and see how strangers react. Don't hide inside, you big chicken!

Temporary dyes are also great for a noticeable, but noncommittal, change. Go for a bright shade that's a big departure from your natural color. Try braids and beads as if you just got back from a Caribbean vacation, or pop on a wig that makes you look and feel like an entirely different person. When you change your hair, you feel more bold, daring, and sexy, and you might bring some of that newfound energy into your love life. Give it a try!

The Thrill of the Unexpected

Romance and surprises go hand in hand. To up the romance in your life, do something unexpected for your husband or loved one: Plan an outing for two where your journey unfolds in stages, one surprising layer at a time. Start off with a mysterious car journey where only you know the destination, and then switch to another type of transportation—maybe a horse-drawn carriage that takes you to a special spot. Once you are there perhaps a bright red canoe will ferry you across to a small island where a violinist awaits. You get the idea. None of this has to be too elaborate—the point is to prolong the journey and create a build-up of anticipation and excitement.

Involve your friends and family in the planning, especially if they can offer unique transportation or can help with driving. Know anyone with a classic car that you can borrow? Try contacting a local auto club or even a luxury car rental agency to find one-of-a-kind transportation for your mystery journey. What about an unusual boat, or an antique two-seater bicycle? Anything goes, so long as you end up alone together in a secluded place to create your own fantastic finale.

Naughty Pearls

White pearls are such a traditional symbol of purity, innocence, and faithfulness. Does that make sexy, black Tahitian pearls a symbol of naughtiness? To me, they do have that sexy, bad-girl aura. I like to think of black pearls as a way I can signal to the world that perhaps I am not as sweet and innocent as I appear.

Needless to say, I'm addicted to black pearls in all forms— earrings, necklaces, and bracelets. I also have my own idea of what it means to wear them—and I wear them often! I put on my stark white pearls when I'm feeling sweet and kind, but I throw on my black pearls when I want to feel a little bit mischievous. Imagine how you would feel switching from your white to your black pearls: Maybe it will make you feel braver when entering the company boardroom; maybe it will make you feel sexier on a dinner date; or perhaps it will give you the swaggering, bad-girl courage to make a move on someone you've longed for. Go ahead—let naughty pearls put you in the mood.

Where the Wind Takes You

I admit it—I think that unplanned travel is a way to instant adventure. If you think that making a secret travel plan as I suggested in #12 is just too much work, here is another fun way to pump up the adventure quotient.

Clear your calendar, pack a small bag, gas up the car, get in, and flip a coin. Heads you turn right out on the main road, tails you turn left. Wherever will it lead?

In my case, if my husband and I turned right, we would head up into the mountains for hiking and a stay in whatever small lodge was available (don't cheat and make reservations ahead of time!). If we turned left, we could drive toward the coast and spend a weekend at the beach in search of perfect seashells. Either way we turned, we would be casting our fates to the wind and driving out into the world with no hotel plan, no restaurant arrangements, and precious little in the way of an agenda.

Who knows where you might end up? Who knows what kind of a quirky hotel you might find? Who knows what type of odd little diner will serve you pie and soup? Who knows what kinds of wacky souvenirs you might end up collecting to remind you of the weekend you turned right, or the weekend you turned left?

Forever a Bride

Want to feel all warm and tingly about how romantic life can be? Pick up a bridal magazine and swoon over the dreamy images in its glossy pages. Why should single girls and brides have all the fun? Even long-married women like me can enjoy reading a bridal magazine. Whether you just want to return to the optimism and the thrill that comes from embarking on a new stage of life or you're simply looking for new entertaining, decorating, and fashion tips, bridal magazines invite you to indulge.

Flip slowly through the pages of smiling brides and starry-eyed grooms, and pretty soon you will start to get all nostalgic thinking about your own big day (and your wedding night, too, of course), no matter how long ago it was. If you get the urge, dust off your wedding album and pore over the images of your first day as a married couple. Ask yourself this—Why shouldn't the rest of my life be as special as my wedding day?

File it Under Romance

Steam up that boring old filing cabinet with a brand new file labeled "romance." Clip and file anything that strikes you as important to your romantic life, whether it's a review of a CD that would be perfect for your next trip down the coast, a magazine photo of a large bed frame you want for the master bedroom, or an article about a hill town in Italy you'd love to visit someday. You might even jot down a few ideas from this book and put them in your romance file to get yourself started!

Here's what I have in my romance folder right now: a recipe for a hotel meal that my husband and I enjoyed on our last vacation, a sketch of a hand-hewn stone patio that I'd like us to build for late-night stargazing, and a review of a downtown restaurant with private booths to cozy up in. We haven't been there yet, but every time I am out of ideas, I just grab the romance file, and suddenly I have an option. Keep your file close at hand, and you'll never be at a loss for ideas!

Special Request

Too many times we put our own needs aside to accommodate everyone else. To get the life you want, sometimes you just have to ask for it. From now on, make a point to express exactly what it is that you need or desire.

In a restaurant, ask the chef to create a special dish for you instead of ordering off the menu. Why not? Ask the woman at airport check-in for an upgrade to first class. Better yet, tell your husband exactly what you'd like him to do to you in bed. Put yourself out there and see what happens!

A few days ago I overheard a woman ask her car mechanic to lower a $400 repair bill: "I've been so faithful in coming to you all these years; do you think you can come down on the price a little?" I was astonished. And he was, too, from the sound of it. What cool courage, and props to her for trying! I have no idea if her bold move worked, but bless her heart for speaking up and asking for something other than what she was offered.

So go ahead, make your feelings known, and chances are, you will be delighted with the outcome.

Speaking in Tongues

Learning to speak to your lover in a foreign language is a really effective way of igniting some passion. You don't have to be fluent; all you need is a few key words. I can personally pull out a few Persian words now and then, come up with a Swedish phrase or two, and say something amusing in French or Spanish. That doesn't mean I could capably hail a cab or order a meal in a foreign country—but for a few dazzling seconds I can appear quite sophisticated in public and quite sexy in the arms of my husband.

What can you add to your foreign language base? Start by studying food and cooking terms—that always comes in handy and makes you appear casually well-traveled in most restaurant situations. Swearing in another language is always impressive too—you can easily pick that up by watching a foreign film or two.

For the truly dedicated a language course with your partner is a great way to invite adventure and romance into your life. Thinking and speaking to each other in a foreign tongue is not just a way to get the sparks flying, but it will also get you dreaming about places you'd love to visit together. Hello Paris! Next stop, Madrid!

Schoolgirl Delights

Sharpen those pencils, sister, and head on back to school! Taking a class is a great way to bond with your man, build confidence in yourself, and open up to new adventures and ideas. Choose a subject that you and your partner would like to learn more about, and sign up for a class. Once you find a topic that truly intrigues you, don't be surprised if you begin to plan trips around your scholarly topic, buy books and research online to learn more, or seek out other people with the same interest you have. My own personal interest involves architecture, and one specific architect from the 1930s named Julia Morgan. Not only do I devour books about her and her colleagues, but I also have a reason to drive around California with my husband seeking out the houses she designed (including Hearst Castle).

What is the best part about being in school together after all these years? Passing notes, late-night study sessions, flirting in the hallways before class, and in general, feeling like a schoolgirl again!

The Pursuit of Elegance

Life in earlier centuries always looks dashing, doesn't it? Bounding over low hedges on horseback, riding sidesaddle in a long flowing skirt, our active ancestors were so much more appealing and romantic than today's spandex-clad gym-goers. To add some old-fashioned elegance to your life, pick up a high-class "exercise" regime like fencing or English riding. You'll be amazed how good it makes you feel about yourself and how that translates to more action in the bedroom!

Fencing helps you learn to move in a streamlined and sinuous way while fending off an attacker. Just think how safe you'll feel knowing that, should another swordsman burst through the window during an office meeting, you'll know exactly what to do. En garde!

English riding can also add a sense of adventure and romance to your life (while firming your butt and thighs). Of course any kind of horseback riding is adventurous, but I'm especially fond of the English-style clothes. I love the way it feels to wander around dressed up like Jackie O about to leave for a foxhunt.

You won't have to look further than the phone book or the Internet to find either a fencing school or a riding academy in your area. Call and enroll in a class so you can steep yourself in adventure and romance.

It Takes Two

Learning the tango is an equally elegant, and downright sexy, alternative to learning how to fence or ride horses. The tango, you may already know, is a hot dance from Argentina that resembles slow, steamy sex. The men hold the women incredibly close, bending and swaying and twirling and dipping on the dance floor.

Find a local dance studio and sign up for classes with your loved one (assuming he's willing), or go to tango night at a local club, just as they do in Latin America! If you or your guy are too shy to tango in public, buy an instructional DVD instead, or throw a tango party just for close friends. My friend Jennifer planned a tango birthday party for herself: She rented a large community center, hired an instructor, and invited her friends to join her for a night of dancing. She knew that learning the dance together with a group of close friends would not be nearly as intimidating as learning at a tango club.

You might end up realizing that it's the music you love most. If so, buy a CD by Astor Piazzolla, one of the true masters of the genre. Tango music is known to arouse passion, so try playing it in the bedroom to set the mood.

A Taste
of the Exotic

Want to venture somewhere new? Invite your partner to join
you for dinner tonight in Brazil, Morocco, Japan, or Turkey. Let
the hardworking restaurateurs, build the sets for your adventure,
and sink into the atmosphere they have so kindly created for
you to enjoy with your dinner. To add to the evening, bring
along a travel book for that particular country, and sit together
enjoying the food and flipping through the pages, choosing
places you'd love to visit someday. If your waiter speaks the language, ask him or her to teach you a few words and phrases!

For an even sexier experience, find a restaurant that lets you
eat with your hands, or one where you can sit on the floor while
you eat: like a formal Japanese restaurant with low tables for
intimate dining or a Middle Eastern restaurant decorated with
swooping curtains and colorful silk pillows. Break out of the
usual steak and potatoes routine and surprise your palate (and
your partner) with some new and adventurous flavors. You may
be just a few blocks from home, but your mind will be miles and
miles away.

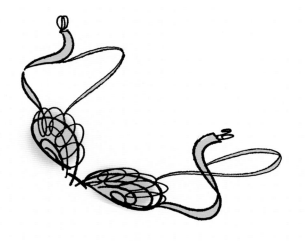

Lingerie Revisited

I have a little ritual when I wash out my bras and lace panties. As I soap, rinse, and soak them in the sink, I think about where they have been and what they have been doing since the last time I washed them. I like to think of it as. . . *The Adventures of My Underwear.*

The next time you hand wash your delicates, let your mind wander back to their most recent adventures. That black lace thing, didn't you wear it dancing last weekend? The push-up bra, wasn't that the one you wore to the PTA meeting to give yourself a secret thrill? You'll be surprised at how much pleasure you'll extract from the formerly mundane task of hand washing your lingerie. While you stop to consider where your lingerie has been, try to imagine where it might be going in the future. . . dream up new places to wear your favorite underthings, and dare to create scenarios about who else might be seeing them.

For romantic inspiration, add a few drops of lavender essential oil to your liquid detergent. It will help you relax and let your imagination drift.

Bedtime Stories

Everyone knows you're supposed to speak up and tell your partner what feels good in bed, but that's a lot easier said than done. Imagine turning to your partner in the middle of dinner to say, "By the way, I really like it when you. . ."

Here is a better way to spice up your sex life: Cuddle up under the covers, and read sex tip books with your partner. The next time things seem a little slow, casually lean over and pick up that book you just happened to find on the nightstand. Read some selections to each other out loud. If your partner hoots at the author's ideas, you won't be as hurt as you would be if it were your own idea.

Here are a few titles for bedroom inspiration (besides the one you're reading right now):

- *Red Hot Tantra*
- *Your Long Erotic Weekend*
- *Mind-Blowing Orgasms Every Day*

To get even more "bang for your buck," take your loved one shopping for the right book. If all goes well, you may have to pull over on the way home from the bookstore!

Household Wonders

We don't normally think of household items as being very sexy, but what if you were to get creative and involve one of them in your sex life? In my living room, for instance, a stack of red silk square pillows sits innocently against the wall, ready and waiting to be used for family game night. But that is not always how those pillows are utilized. . .Let's just say they have supported me in a variety of nighttime positions.

On occasion, when I'm entertaining company and the pillow stack catches my eye across the living room, I smile and remember nights when they were put to their less innocent use. It gives me quite a charge to think that something sitting there in full view for anyone to see plays a frequent role in my love life.

So. . .what other household items can you naughtily incorporate into your own erotic life? An innocent-looking footstool, perhaps? The little lap blanket you keep on the couch? The kitchen counter? Why not use that new pastry brush to apply some body paint? One thing's for sure, you'll never look at your pastries the same way again!

Enjoyable
Read

Millions of women read romance novels to get themselves in the mood. The best historical romance novels reveal all about love and sex hundreds of years ago—so they can also offer useful ideas and romantic insights. So pick one up, and let the printed word rev you up and teach you a thing or two about romance.

Bridget Jones is your soul sister, I know; but in *The Volcano Lover*, Emma Hamilton can teach you how to capture the heart and body of a famous war hero when his ship docks in your town. The well-read young prostitute "Sugar" in the novel *The Crimson Petal and the White* will let you in on the frank desires of Victorian Englishmen, and the crafty courtesan who cavorts on the pages of *In the Company of the Courtesan* will teach you new ways to smuggle jewels out of a war-torn city. Lifting up long skirts to see what was (or was not) going on underneath them is a fun obsession for modern folks.

Sink back into the pillows of your bed with a glowing candle nearby, a glass of port in hand, and a sultry song playing on the stereo while you explore another world and come up with clever ways to bring some of that world into your own. . . .

Something's Cooking

Taking a cooking class with your significant other is a fun way to get your hearts pumping in the kitchen. Skip the dull and ordinary courses on "How to Feed a Family of Four in Five Minutes," and instead opt for a class on international cuisine. Many adult learning organizations offer international cooking courses that can teach you to cook your way around the globe with sushi, crepes, or schnitzel.

Not only will that course on French country cooking open you both up to a new world of wine and sausages, but it might also lead to the beginnings of a plan to actually visit the source! Getting your hands dirty together in the kitchen is always a way to draw closer, and doing so in a group setting brings a sense of teamwork and solidarity that you may not have felt in a while. It's a powerful way to renew your sense of each other as a couple.

Change
of Plans

Anticipation before a trip is thrilling indeed. What if it turned out that the vacation you anticipated was a ruse from the beginning? What if you were told the plan was skiing for the weekend, only to show up with your bags and learn that the plane was headed for Bermuda instead? Who knew life could be so full of surprises?

While you could simply ask your partner to plan a switcheroo trip for you, it's not as fun if you know it's coming. Better to plan one for him and let him return the favor someday. So here's your tactic: Plan a trip for you and your loved one, but don't tell all. It will then be your responsibility to secretly bring along (or ship) all of the right wardrobe and equipment for whatever you have planned.

Not every guy will be amused by this little adventure trick. If you have promised to arrange his dream skiing vacation only to surprise him with a cruise, someone might end up crying (and it might be you). But if your partner likes a good joke and is easy-going about how events unfold, then give this sneaky travel method a try! Teach him that you're a woman of adventure and make a silent vow to always keep him guessing.

Admit Two

For some good old-fashioned romance, why not go on a good-old-fashioned date? Head to an antique or antique-style movie theatre, get a giant bucket of popcorn to share, and snuggle up to your loved one to watch a classic black-and-white film. The less popular the movie, the better, as it will give you a chance to feel that teenage thrill of being all alone together in the dark. Even in a crowded theatre, there's nothing to stop you from engaging in a little cuddling or a good, healthy make-out session. Who cares if the granny behind you grunts her stern disapproval—that only adds to the fun! If you're really shy, find two seats in the back row where you can enjoy extra privacy.

Chances are, you'll leave the theatre arm in arm, having seen very little of the movie. If you did manage to catch a few key scenes, look for a quaint coffee shop or diner where you can hold hands across the table and rehash the most romantic parts.

Use Your Hands

Look around at the people you know—doesn't it seem like those with the most interesting and adventuresome lives are the folks with a hands-on, creative outlet? It's the corporate lawyer who stays up late at night practicing violin, the nurse whose garden is filled with clay sculptures she fashions herself, or the teacher with a wall full of drawings she has made of her students over the years.

Experience how sensual it can be to work and create with your hands. It doesn't matter if you are any good. What matters is the very physical thrill of using that part of your body in a whole new way—to hold a charcoal pencil; to shape a mound of wet clay; to press the keys of a piano; to spread fingerpaints across a grainy canvas—anything that's an attempt to create your own version of beauty.

Drawing is a great way to get started, because anyone can do it—all you need is a good drawing pencil and a sketchpad. You don't have to show it to anyone! Just like the thrill of writing secret erotica, producing your own secret art can be as private a matter as you choose. If you're feeling bold, sign up for a life drawing class, alone or with your partner. Learn how to appreciate the human form of your live model, and then practice at home with your true love as the subject!

Emergency Romance Kit

31

The secret to romance: Never fail to pull over for a beautiful sunset or a breathtaking view, but plan ahead so you don't have to enjoy it empty-handed. How many times have you pulled over with your loved one to share a moment and thought, *If only we had a glass of wine in hand*? Never again! Put together an emergency romance road kit—complete with a bottle of wine—to enhance life's perfect moments.

First invest in a padded wine carrier and some heavy plastic wine glasses—there's nothing romantic about finding broken glass in the trunk of your car. Next comes the wine. Choose something modestly priced that doesn't need to be served chilled— something that will add just a touch of elegance to the moment. Add a heavy old quilt or an army blanket to your emergency romance collection, and perhaps small folding chairs if you prefer to stay off the ground. And don't forget the wine bottle opener, or you might have another emergency on your hands!

Musical by Nature

32

Going to the theatre or the opera house is lovely, but there's also something wonderfully freeing and slightly more romantic about sitting in the grass under the sun or the moon for a live musical performance. The kind that you stumble upon is the best kind of all, because it turns an otherwise ordinary moment into a more memorable one.

If you're looking for something more deliberate, check with the Chamber of Music in your town and see if there are any free, outdoor performances coming up. Perhaps a folk band plays every week at your local farmers' market. I make up a list of all the free outdoor performances that happen in our town during the warmer months and keep it posted on the fridge for spur-of-the-moment, romantic outings with my husband.

If you don't mind paying for tickets, there might also be a nearby venue that takes advantage of a natural setting. No matter how you find your outdoor concert or performance, plop yourself down on the grass, lean back, close your eyes, and enjoy this unique, sensory experience.

Long Flowing Skirts

A glance out the window confirms your worst fears: It looks like
another gloomy, cloudy day in which nothing will happen. It
doesn't have to be that way, though. To transform a humdrum
day into one that makes you feel like you're on your way to pose
for a Gainsborough painting, or like someone who has a car sent
for them wherever they go: Pull on a long skirt. Not a formal
skirt, mind you—no velvet or satin this early in the day, but a
long flowing wool skirt or a crinkly washed silk that brushes
against your legs and ankles as you walk down the hallway at
work. Choose something you can pair with boots for an added
bit of sophistication.

Dressing in a romantic outfit lets the world know you have
softer things in mind than the harsh world in which we live.
Strangers will wonder who that elegant woman is in the floating
cloud of fabric. Your friends and family will wonder what exactly
is on your mind—are you off to spend the day writing poetry or
to paint a landscape in a grassy field? And most importantly, *you*
will think of yourself in a more romantic way. Perhaps you *will*
spend your day painting and running through fields!

A Touch of the Islands

34

Did you honeymoon in Hawaii? Do you *wish* you honeymooned in Hawaii? Here is your chance to create a bit of aloha spirit in your daily life on the mainland: Give your man a lei.

Special order a lei online (www.hawaiiflowerlei.com) or ask your local florist to special order it for you. You can buy a braided ti leaf lei (very masculine) to drape over his shoulders on a special evening at home; and why not pick up a fragrant one for yourself at the same time? Fire up the blender for some fruity tropical drinks, put on a little slack key guitar Hawaiian music, and have your own private hula.

One thing's for sure: The more you can evoke a wild night on the beach, the more willing he'll be to bring that fantasy to life.

Go Public

The more you think about sex, the more you'll have it, right? Absolutely! Why not be daring and record your sexiest, most intimate thoughts in your very own online diary? Throw away that old-fashioned journal you've been keeping and start an erotic blog. With a blog you can use tawdry graphics and feel the tingly anticipation that if you make it public, anyone in the world (including your mother-in-law and your first grade teacher!) can read it.

If you're nervous, start out with one that's private. Register and create your blog on a free site like www.blogger.com and begin making daily or weekly entries. Maybe you'll write about your wildest sexual fantasies, things you've always wanted to try. Maybe you'll create a make-believe sex life for yourself, spinning wild tales of things you only wish you'd actually experienced. Once you're comfortable with blogging and have written a few solid entries, it's time to share your secret with your loved one. Imagine the surprise on his face! Encourage him to start his own site so you can share and compare entries.

If you're feeling even bolder and want to satisfy that exhibitionist side, go public with your erotic blog and show your raciest thoughts and dreams to the world! Just don't be surprised if you get a frantic call from your mother-in-law.

Romance Party with Friends

So far I've been amusing you (I hope) with ideas on romantic evenings and encounters for you and that special someone in your life. But why hog all of this romance energy to yourselves? Why not invite some other happy couples to add to or share in the warmth?

Valentine's Day is an ideal time to host a few other couples for an evening at your place, but you can also celebrate your anniversary among friends. Here is how to put everyone in a fun and loving mood for your party—instead of ordinary name tags, assign everyone a new identity for the evening. Re-christen them as pairs of famous lovers—Romeo and Juliet, Robin Hood and Marian, Bogie and Bacall, Joe and Marilyn, William Randolph Hearst and his beloved Marion, Antony and Cleopatra, and anyone else you can think of! Be sure and save your favorite pair for yourself and your love, of course.

Leave notorious bickerers off your invite list; they'll just spoil the fun and make everyone else uncomfortable. Stick with couples who actually get along and try to invite at least one newly formed or newly married couple—watching them fawn over each other may bring back some fond memories. Remember when you were so sweet and attentive to each other? "Awwwww".

Elevate the Mundane

Both at work and at home, our lives are too consumed with the ordinary. From sunup to sundown, we spend our time making sandwiches, answering the phone, picking socks off the floor, and attending meetings (hopefully not all at the same time). How do we awaken ourselves from the daily routines that sap the surprise and romance out of our lives? We find small ways to add enjoyment to these mundane tasks until they transform into something almost inspiring.

I add a bit of oomph and romance to my day using music, scents, and decorative touches. Soft classical music played in the background of my office helps me stay calm and adds a small measure of beauty to my daily environment. A squirt of lavender linen spray on my sheets at night relaxes my body and adds an atmosphere of luxury and elegance to my otherwise ordinary bedtime routine. Wearing a long, swoopy strand of pearls while vacuuming makes it seem like I'm living an entirely different sort of life (one in which the maid didn't show up and I have to clean before the ambassador arrives for cocktails!).

How can you boost what you do on a daily basis? Be creative about how you make a task a tiny bit different, a tiny bit special, and a tiny bit new.

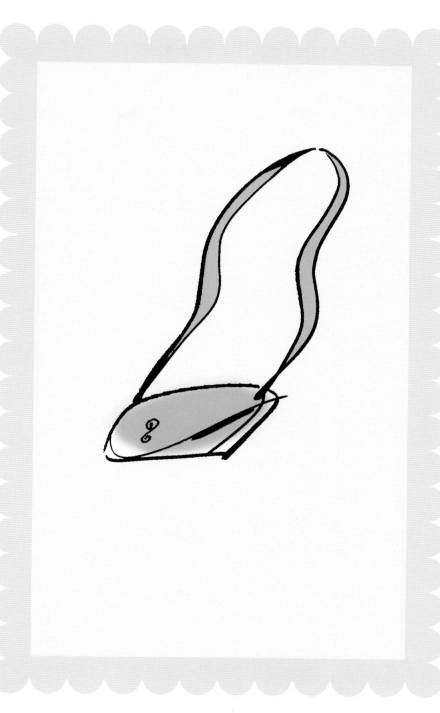

Rise and Shine

Yes, leaving your head on the pillow an extra hour in the morning is a luxury indeed, but think of how much you miss in life while you are asleep! So much action and adventure awaits the early bird, particularly one that doesn't *usually* get up that early!

What could you be doing so early in the morning? You could visit a farmers' market, run on a deserted road, walk in the crisp morning air, or do yoga outdoors without anyone watching. Imagine the beauty of a sunrise hike!

Once a month I get up at 4:00 a.m. and sell antiques from a rented booth at a local fair. The doors open to the public at 6:30 a.m., and I have to say that all of the most interesting things happen in the earliest hours. Not long ago at about 7:00 a.m. I watched a couple test-ride an antique tandem bike. They wobbled precariously through the aisles giggling while most of the town slept. They didn't buy the bike, but will they remember the morning they took that goofy ride? Absolutely.

Set your alarm tomorrow, and get a glimpse of what happens early in the day. What a great sense of achievement you can feel from experiencing a small adventure before most rational folk are even awake!

Love Bites

Seems odd that the very dinners we prepare for a romantic evening at home, or order on a special night out—steaks, cheesecakes, pastas—are those meals most likely to sit in our tummies for hours afterward like lumps of clay, making us much less interested in doing the deed for which we were setting the stage. It's hard to feel sexy when you feel soooo full, isn't it?

Why not prepare a light supper as sexy foreplay, then? Let him in on the plan; tell him exactly what you have in mind for later and that to be in tip-top shape, you are making a light dinner of fresh veggies and fish. That evening he will happily eat the kind of meal that would otherwise annoy him. Who knew salad could ever be sexy? Give it a try.

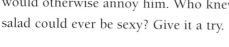

A Fresh Face

Sometimes the sexiest touch is the simplest change you can make. For instance, every makeup artist knows that adding a small bit of frosted gloss in the center of your made-up lips makes them look that much more kissable. To feel renewed and attract more attention than ever before, make one small change to your ordinary makeup or jewelry.

Apply some blush and mascara if you usually go natural; wear earrings and a necklace if you normally wouldn't. If you tend to use everything in your (slightly overstuffed) cosmetics case, dare to use only a dot of moisturizer today. Be forewarned that your partner may not notice the change you make. If he does, consider it a bonus—the real reward is that *you* will feel like a slightly different, slightly sexier person, open to exploring a new side of yourself. Notice how this change to your appearance has an effect on your behavior. Do you walk with more of a swing to your step? Do you smile wider to show off that bright red lipstick? Will you say hello to just about everyone in the office today?

Castles in the Clouds

Having a castle of your own wouldn't be such a bad thing, would it? Sure, it would be drafty and difficult to heat, but hey, what a problem to have! Or you could just go and visit someone else's castle, imagining that it's your own. There's an amazing castle in Italy called Galeazza that hosts a reading retreat. Wouldn't it be lovely to curl up with a book in the library of a castle for a week or two? Daydream on their site at www.galeazza.com. Or book a stay at one of the many beautiful castles in Scotland, England, Ireland, and Wales. Check out www.celticcastles.com, my queen, and pick your favorite.

For a romantic castle adventure closer to home, consider touring New York's Castle on the Hudson, Washington state's Thornewood Castle, or California's luxurious Hearst Castle.

This site lists castles by state, so you might even find one near your hometown:

www.dupontcastle.com/castles

If you can't get to a real castle anytime soon, sit down in the sand and ask your love to help you build one. Even the playful act of trying to build a sand castle before the tide ruins your efforts is a fun way to spend the afternoon.

Appeal to His Masculine Senses

Fond as my husband, Peter, is of classical music, he winces at my endless use of it both in and out of the bedroom. To really get your loved one's blood flowing, sometimes you have to change the music to something romantic yet masculine. Sound impossible? Not really. What about the theme songs to '60s spaghetti westerns played on a cello? What man wouldn't think it was romantically inspiring to hear the theme song from *The Good, The Bad, and The Ugly* playing in his bedroom late at night? How about the deep, sexy sound of Johnny Cash?

Perhaps the theme music to *Pirates of the Caribbean* will get his heart racing as he closes his eyes and imagines himself as a swaggering pirate come to town for a bit of pillaging. The sound track to the big-ships-at-sea movie *Master and Commander* is also filled with music that will make his heart race. Keep any or all of these CDs in your bedroom to set the mood and make things more rough and tough than Wolfgang Mozart ever was. Your loved one will appreciate your wholehearted attempt to appeal to his tastes, and you'll both enjoy the thrill of moving your bodies to a new rhythm.

Be a
Survivor

To truly live a life of adventure, you will need to develop an ability to overcome life's little challenges. If you are self-reliant and skilled, you will not only be able to handle these challenges—but you will also be more open to embarking on adventures in the first place.

Take the time to get at least a few survival skills under your belt: Learn how to build a fire, start a balky car, or perform CPR. That way when a minor catastrophe strikes, you'll encounter it head on, with confidence. Can you read a map? Do you know how to work a compass? Build a shelter? Find edible plants? Even city girls might someday find themselves in a wacky situation where they need to step in and be heroic. Will you be up for the challenge? All it takes is a willingness to learn.

Make a list of survival skills that you would like to acquire, and then select one to work on over the next few weeks. Maybe your partner would like to learn alongside you so that you will both be in an adventurous mindset, ready to apply your newfound skills in a wild, uninhabited setting.

Chart
Your Course

Tired of all those posters and family photos hanging on your walls? Need a fun reminder that your life can be one of exotic romance and adventure, and not just everyday sameness? As a symbol of your new, more adventurous life, decorate your home with a framed map of a location you dream of exploring.

Find something big and bold, not a little thing you would stash in your glove compartment. Look for a beautiful map with artistic qualities, perhaps something antique that shows your favorite location some decades or centuries ago. Since maps are inexpensive, why not spring for a really gorgeous one or an impressive frame to set it in?

Finding smaller maps is as easy as perusing old travel books at your local used bookstores. I found a really cool rendering of Southeast Asia in the 1920s in an old travel book and hung it in my bathroom—that small gesture has planted the seed for a future trip to Thailand, Malaysia, or Singapore! You might also want to honor a past trip by framing a map of the dreamiest place you've ever visited. Did you spend your honeymoon in Venice strolling hand in hand? Hang a map of the city in your entryway, and each time you enter or leave your home, the memories will come rushing back.

Message in a Bottle

Need to let someone know that they really rock your world, but feeling a tad too shy to actually say it? Send a subtle message with a wine bottle label—a bottle of Earthquake Zin, for instance.

Wine store shelves are filled with quirky and provocative names that express all kinds of emotions (if you're creative enough to interpret them). In a sexy mood? Why not promise an amazing evening by presenting your man with a bottle of Seven Deadly Zins? Or send a secret message to a crush with a bottle of Incognito (a stark black bottle with a simple gold mask on it). One California vintner even markets a wine called Ménage a Trois, should that be a message you would someday like to send. . . .

Don't despair if your wine label message doesn't come through loud and clear the first time around. Some guys aren't attuned to subtlety. Simply let him in on the game you're playing, and soon he'll be playing it, too. Send him a new message every Friday night over dinner, or send one to his office every month. Use this opportunity to say what you're too darned shy to admit. Plus, it's fun to spend the day at the wine shop cruising the aisles, searching for something that expresses your deepest thoughts and urges.

Poster Girl

Marilyn Monroe was once the standard against which all women measured themselves. They wanted that smooth, breathy voice; that girlish charm; those luscious curves; that platinum blonde hair; and those plump red lips. She was the embodiment of sex, so why not take a page out of her book? One of Marilyn Monroe's most memorable performances occurred when she wiggled out onto stage in a tight white gown and breathlessly sang the *Happy Birthday* song to President John F. Kennedy. Imagine recreating this famous moment for your own beloved! Her voice was just a whisper, so use your best sexy, breathy voice when singing.

If you're not much of a performer, you can emulate Marilyn's classic elegance in other ways. Buy a pair of high-heeled marabou bedroom slippers—extra fluffy—and wear them around the house with a white silk negligee or bathrobe. Paint your lips a shocking shade of red to complete the image. Spread yourself out on the couch or bed and imagine that you are a celebrity in your own home. Treasure the look on your loved one's face when he walks in the door and is greeted by the ghost of Marilyn!

Eyes in All Directions

You're sitting in your car, staring straight ahead at the light, just waiting for it to turn green. What might you be missing to the left and to the right while your eyes are set in one direction? I'm using a metaphor here, of course, but too many of us keep our eyes focused forward and fail to see the opportunities and adventures all around us. So look to the left; look to the right. Explore. Act on your natural sense of curiosity and peer under life's carpet to see what's there.

I spend a lot of time reading those little flyers and notes that people post on telephone poles and billboards all over. It keeps me aware of all the quirky little things happening in my town. Recently I went to a theatre benefit that started at 10:30 at night (when the actors were done with their other performances). I saw Tommy Tune, the famous Broadway star, in a small theatre setting where he entertained a crowd of only fifty people. Where had I learned about it? From an odd little flyer that I'd accepted from a stranger. Similarly, one of my cousins spotted a tiny sign on a country road that said "casting." She stopped, out of curiosity, and ended up with a role in a Steven Spielberg movie!

The next time you spot something out of the corner of your eye, don't ignore it. It could be your next big adventure!

The Other City of Love

Feeling too poor for Paris, but want to enjoy the romance of French culture? A delightful international experience is available just a few hours north of the U.S. border, in the most French part of Canada: Quebec City. The oldest city in North America, Quebec City is also the only remaining walled city, with thick stone walls surrounding the Old Town to protect against invaders. Immerse yourself in the culture of Quebec, and spend your time there speaking the language, drinking the wine, eating in outdoor cafés, and strolling cobblestone streets.

Chances are the price of the best hotel in Paris would seriously stretch your finances, but the best hotel in Quebec City, Fairmont Le Chateau Frontenac, has rooms starting at $299 Canadian (www.fairmont.com). Built by the Canadian Pacific Railway in the late nineteenth century, Chateau Frontenac is a towering stone castle located inside the fortified section of Quebec City, close to many museums, cafés, and galleries. The city is also filled with less expensive and equally charming accommodations.

Remember to learn at least a few key French phrases before you go, especially ones like, "What wine do you recommend?"; "Does this negligee come in black?"; and "More chocolate crepes, please."

Incognito

Wearing a mask gives us all the temporary courage to flirt, to be a bit wild, and to let loose and behave in ways we wouldn't if we had to show our faces. Seize upon any opportunity you have to dress up like another person and put a mysterious mask over your eyes. If it's not even close to Halloween, consider throwing a costume party or a masquerade ball for you and as many friends as you can fit in your home. Keep a supply of cheap, colorful masks, feather boas, funny glasses, and various hats at the door, for those who dare to come as themselves.

How do you get your own man to wear a costume? Let him look like his usual self but with a subtle twist! I once got my husband to go to a Halloween costume party as a Wall Street trader wearing his usual business suit. All I did was stuff fake stocks and bonds in his breast pocket. Is your loved one most comfortable in a plaid shirt and boots—hello sexy lumberjack!

Here is the real secret behind dressing in costume—you not only feel like a different person in a costume or mask, but you *are* a different person for a few delicious hours, and it can carry on into the bedroom later that night (another way to convince him to dress up).

Hip-notize Him

Ever seen a real belly dancer in action, her healthy, curvy form gyrating in wave-like motions? Belly dancing isn't just a dance—it's an entire fantasy world of breezy costumes, sparkling jewelry, and exotic music. How can you be part of this world and learn these super sensuous moves? Sign up for a belly dancing class in your area. If you can't find one, go online for beginner belly dance DVDs and videos at sites like www.bellydanceshoppe.com. To get yourself in the right frame of mind, throw on a long skirt, some hoop earrings, and a top that shows off your midriff, and start working those hips.

Belly dancing is believed to give you sexual power. And here's the best part: You don't have to be a super-slim showgirl to harness that power. In fact, the most popular belly dancers have a bit of a tummy roll—all the better to show off their moves. So no matter what your body type, there's no reason why you can't get out there and dance. Learning to move your body in a new, provocative way will help you feel sensual later on when you have an audience of one. Because, of course, you have to belly dance for him!

Make Music Together

Music has a way of transporting us back to key moments in our lives and in our developing relationships. What song was playing when you shared your first kiss? What song did you dance to at your wedding? Maybe Mozart reminds you of your first home together, because it was playing on the radio the day you drove to the open house. Here's an easy way to relive those warm and magical moments anytime you feel the need:

Put together a CD or cassette tape collection of your relationship's "Greatest Hits." Include songs that you both simply love in addition to ones that commemorate a key moment in your relationship. Bring it with you on a long road trip, play it softly at work to make you think of him, pop it in the stereo at home to get you both in a romantic mood, or play it after a big fight to help you remember why you love him so deeply. Need an excuse to make your musical collection? I can't think of a better Valentine's Day or anniversary gift!

In the Nude

52

When vowing to live a more romantic life, one filled with more spice and adventure, you should probably include your body in your plans, don't you think? It is a fairly critical element.

One of the key ingredients for a happy and healthy sex life is a good body image. We all have body parts and imperfections that we'd love to change, but focusing on these figure flaws does our love life no good. Want to become more comfortable in your own skin? Exercise is, of course, one good way to do it, but here's another technique:

Spend more time in the nude. In fact, why not spend time being naked every day! I'm not just talking about the few seconds it takes to slip on a new set of clothes. Spend a whole morning or evening walking around the house making coffee, watching television, or reading a magazine in the buff (be sure to shut the shades first, though). Enjoy feeling the air on your bare skin as you learn to relax with the body you have now. After a while, you may even forget that you're naked! When you start to feel more comfortable, see if you can get your partner to join you in your naked sessions. Just make sure that your kids are out of the house—you don't want to scar them forever!

Finger Foods

Picture this: It's a quiet dinner for two in an intimate setting. You gaze across the table at your love, dip a luscious morsel of food into butter and offer it up to his mouth, letting him lick and suck the juice off your fingers. What's on the menu here? Crab and lobster, two of the sexiest finger foods around. Hint: If you serve it at home, you can even take your finger food feast one step further and eat it naked except for the plastic bib! No giggling, now.

Crab and lobster are not only delicious, but they are also natural aphrodisiacs that inspire lovemaking. So why not use them as the centerpiece for an entire home-cooked meal of "love foods"? Tomatoes were called "love apples" in years past because they were thought of as sexy. Raw oysters are another popular food thought to enhance sexual performance. Their slippery texture, alone, inspires thoughts of favorite body parts.

Shop together for an entire spread of aphrodisiacs and you'll be amazed at how quickly dinner is served.

Scotch by the Fire

What man wouldn't want to snuggle up in front of the fire with you if you poured him a big glass of good Scotch? Sometimes we need to cater to a man's unique tastes in order to get the warmth and togetherness we crave, don't we? Invest in a bottle of single malt Scotch like Oban or Balvenie to awaken his senses. To go along with your special bottle, buy two beautiful lead crystal drink glasses to bring out for this special occasion. Build the fire, put the kids to bed, turn on your favorite music, pour your drinks, and settle in for the night.

If you're not fond of drinking straight liquor, try mixing together something a little bit tastier. To make a cocktail called a MacDougall, simply add two teaspoons of lime juice and one teaspoon of Grenadine to two ounces of Scotch. Shake with ice, strain it, and then pour your drink into a fancy glass with some ice and a twist of lime.

Seek out similar opportunities to enjoy Scotch when you're traveling, and always ask if your hotel room, or at least the hotel bar, has a fireplace. That way you'll be warm and toasty from the inside out.

Share a Hobby

Most couples are like us—they have separate hobbies. In my marriage, I needlepoint, and my husband watches trains. Neither of us plans to take the other's hobby up anytime soon. So what can we do together that will interest us both? Developing a common interest in collecting is a wonderful and fulfilling way to spend more time together. You might choose to collect art (imagine how much fun you could have collecting erotic art), autographs, cars, or books on a particular topic that intrigues you both (maybe you could build your own library of Kama Sutra books!).

My husband's family has collected Rookwood pottery for four generations, and through my husband's influence I, too, managed to fall under the spell. Now that we have this quest in common, my husband and I use the search for Rookwood to travel to auctions, cruise museums, and visit other collectors together.

How will you decide what to collect? What a good excuse to sit down with your loved one and discuss your shared interests over wine.

Made by Hand

The next time you feel like expressing your feelings for your love, don't spend the money on a preprinted greeting card with a sappy poem that someone else wrote. Make your very own expressions of love and caring instead.

Making a card can be as simple as folding a sheet of paper in half and tracing the shape of a leaf on the front for a cover (or gluing on a leaf or pressed flower). Even a child-like attempt with crayons or colored markers will carry more personal meaning than a store-bought design.

If you don't feel up to designing a card or writing an entire poem, compose a short, sweet note and attach it to something you've found in the garden. Wash off a small rock and tie on a message about how he "rocks your world." Gather a bunch of leaves before his next business trip and write a message about how you miss him when he "leaves." You get the idea. And once he sees your creativity in bloom, he may be inspired to make the same kind of effort.

Love and Laughter

What happens when you and your lover laugh together? Your tension dissolves; whatever drove you crazy just a few short minutes ago now doesn't seem like such a big deal, and life is grand. Shared laughter makes you feel close, and every warm smile you exchange with each other is money in the romance bank.

So finding ways to laugh together should be a priority, shouldn't it? From seeking out comedy clubs and silly new theatre pieces to spending time with your most hilarious friends and watching the latest and dopiest comedy films, what better way to lighten things up?

Set aside one night of the week for "Comedy Night" and rent old funny movies (perhaps the ones you loved in high school) or old black and white movies with Charlie Chaplin or The Three Stooges, filled with ridiculous pratfalls and physical comedy to keep you giggling all night. Why not make it two nights a week?

If the last thing on your lips every night is a smile instead of a frown, life will be long and happy!

The King's Mistress

58

I recently came across a book at a used bookstore entitled *Sex with Kings* that describes the lives of various royal mistresses. Well, according to this book, the most successful royal mistress "catered" to each of the king's five senses. She was ready to converse gaily with him when she was tired, make love until all hours when she was ill, cater to his every whim, serve his favorite foods, sympathize when he was cranky, massage his feet, decorate his homes—and all with a cheerful demeanor. Doesn't that sound like fun?

Well, what about this instead: What if you pretended to be a royal mistress for just one short day (or heck, a few short hours)? Why not give yourself over for a limited time to focusing exclusively on your lover's needs? Go ahead; cater to all five of his senses. Put on his favorite outfit so he can enjoy the sight of you. Apply some vanilla scented body lotion to his shoulders and begin to massage him while playing his favorite music on the stereo. You get the picture. Just make sure he knows what it is you are doing, though, so you get full credit for giving this a go.

And then make sure he knows that soon it will be *his* turn to play the queen's lover for a few thrilling hours, when he has to cater exclusively to all of *your* five senses! It will all have been worth it.

A Dash of Spice

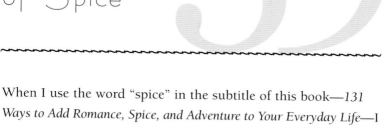

When I use the word "spice" in the subtitle of this book—*131 Ways to Add Romance, Spice, and Adventure to Your Everyday Life*—I mean it as a euphemism for sexiness. But you can also use actual spices to invigorate your life.

How? Make spice a theme in your travels, and visit old spice countries like Indonesia, India, and China to steep yourself in their very romantic history. Or you could focus on a single spice like saffron or cardamom and devote a special themed dinner party to it. If you don't have the nerve to throw a spice-themed party, perhaps just serve a side dish to give everyone something to talk about. Here is a recipe from a famous sixteenth-century Arab sex manual, *The Perfumed Garden*, that is supposed to be an aphrodisiac: Boil green peas and onions, and then spice them with cayenne pepper, cinnamon, ginger, and cardamom. You could also serve it without mentioning its alleged powers and see if there is any result. . . .

Take Care
of Yourself

You do know how to take care of yourself, don't you? You're a big girl; you know what I'm hinting. In the pursuit of adventure, romance, and particularly spice, you sometimes need to. . . pursue your own pleasure. My own personal method involves AA batteries, so I make sure I never run low on them.

Here is the thing about self-pleasure, the ultimate form of self-indulgence: There is no reason to ever be embarrassed, ashamed, or even reluctant to talk about it with your partner. In fact, he will think it is kind of sexy that you bring it up. He will think it is even sexier if you show him!

So go ahead and get spicy on your own, and don't be afraid to tell your partner about it. Pleasing yourself on a regular basis is an important part of a healthy sex life—and I know you want to be as healthy as possible.

Don't Blow Your Money

I'm shocked by the goofy ways people spend money, only to have raging arguments with their spouses about their spending that sabotages otherwise close relationships. Ask any marriage counselor, and they'll tell you that money fights are at the root of most tension between couples. Maybe this is something you already know too well.

We can all agree that the less time you spend fighting about money, the more fun, romance, and adventure you can enjoy. How do you avoid the constant money spats that kill all inklings of romance? Sit down with your partner, once and for all, and set some money rules that you both can live with. Whether you decide on an amount that cannot be exceeded without permission from your partner, or you both assign yourselves a strict monthly budget, you will at least feel hopeful about having created a game plan. The part that comes next, though, is the most important: Stick to the rules you have agreed upon. Otherwise, you'll fall back into the same rut of endless arguments.

Want an inventive way to curb his spending habits? Come up with a sexy reward for every hundred dollars he saves a month. Always keep in mind that material things don't equal happiness, and remember that a simpler life makes you more flexible and able to lead an adventurous life!

Make
Heat

62

If movies are any indication, chiles and sex go well together: In the French film *Chocolat*, the main character whips up a special hot chocolate that her customers and their lovers simply can't get enough of. The secret ingredient: chile. Another sexy, chile-infused movie is *Woman on Top*, with Penelope Cruz as the sexy host of a television cooking show called "Passion Foods." Does the name of that last movie give you an idea of the power of chile? Watch these films together on a hot summer night with the windows open and a warm breeze blowing through. Or cut right to the chase and serve up some raw oysters with habanero hot sauce (habaneros are an intensely spicy chile pepper) or a French onion soup with ancho chile (ancho chile peppers range from sweet to moderately spicy) so that you and your loved one can feel their power firsthand.

Serving hot dishes that bring a bead of sweat to the upper lip can be an exciting suggestion of how hot your night can become later on. But be warned—keep those fiery chiles away from sensitive parts of the body!

Early
Sparks

The first few days, weeks, and months of a new relationship are heaven, so charged with excitement and newness. But has it been a while since you felt that way about your longtime love? Well, why not try to recapture some of that feeling by going back to where you first started out? The first time you and your current partner felt something, was it at an Indian restaurant? Then fill the air with curry! Did you fall in love at an ice rink? Strap on those skates again and get out there on the ice together! My husband and I played Scrabble on our first serious date. Whenever I'm feeling far away from those early feelings of tenderness, I haul out the Scrabble board so we can relive it again. I can still get him excited when I slap down the tiles, but he is even more excited when he wins (which he does a lot).

So go back in time. . .were you a cheerleader watching your football boyfriend out on the field? Go to a game and sit in the stands and reminisce. Afterward you can park your car in front of your house and reenact some of your early romance without worrying that your folks are watching out the window. Wait, that was all part of the fun! On second thought, park in front of your parents' house!

The Kindest Words

Are you as polite as you could be to your husband? Is he as polite as you'd like him to be? Good manners and signs of respect go a long way toward creating a harmonious and romantic household. It is hard to feel warm toward someone who treats you rudely, or in an offhand manner.

How can you change things if you feel badly treated? Speak up, and speak up right away. Simply say, "I think we should be more polite toward one another" or "I feel more romantic when you treat me like a lady." Old-fashioned? Heck yes, but well worth going back in time on this one. I highly recommend the book *Essential Manners for Couples* by Peter Post, of the etiquette family.

Here is the simple formula: Better behaved, better treasured, better relationship = better romance. See how that works?

Soaking
Wet

I always thought the fireplace in my parents' bedroom was the most romantic thing I'd ever seen. But now I'm fonder of the sunken hot tub in our own bathroom, where my husband and I can sit and soak and gaze out at the stars in the quiet parts of the evening.

Who cares if you don't have a big tub for two at your house? There are plenty of options for getting wet and wild. Why not shower together every now and then? If you've got more time on your hands, squeeze into your regular sized bathtub together and enjoy a long soak. Sure it may be a tight fit, but doesn't that just mean you'll have to slip-slide around a little more in the nude? The worst thing that could happen is that you'll erupt into laughter. The best scenario: You'll wedge yourself between your lover's legs, lean back, and take turns washing the other. If you'd rather hold out for the luxury of a bigger tub, book a spa suite at a local hotel, or take a trip just for the excuse of enjoying your own private whirlpool bath. One caution, though: you just might be too relaxed for lovemaking afterward and instead both fall right to sleep!

Work Up a Sweat

Our lives are surrounded by high-tech conveniences, tools, and gadgets that do almost everything for us. While we enjoy the convenience this brings to our modern life, we miss out on the satisfaction that can be had through good old-fashioned hard work. To add an extra touch of adventure and maybe even romance in your life, all you have to do is work up a sweat together. Rake some leaves, paint the house, shovel a little snow, plant a garden, chop some wood, build a shed together—anything to get the blood pumping! Wear as little clothes as you can get away with, and once you're finished, hop right into the pool or a nearby lake to celebrate your accomplishments. You'll be surprised at how exhilarated you feel!

If there's no work to be done (and I find that hard to believe), get out and exercise together. Ride bikes, hit the gym, play tennis, go for a brisk walk, or toss around a football. Exercise can work miracles on your sex drive—not to mention its ability to reduce stress levels and improve your self-image. Resist the temptation to shower when you get home, and enjoy each other in all your natural glory!

Healing Hands

In the quiet moments in our house after the two boys have gone to bed, my husband and I try to do a little something together before we settle down under the covers with our separate books and carefully adjusted reading lamps. We indulge in a slippery massage by the fire.

Picture this scene in your home on a winter night: The fire is lit, the children are sleeping (soundly, you hope), and you and your love are together in front of the fireplace with a bottle of massage lotion. Sometimes all it takes is a glance over at the massage supplies that are casually lined up next to the fireplace, and I am already relaxed and feeling romantic. Who gets to have a massage, and who gets to give a massage? I do hope you'll be fair and switch off on a regular basis. Why not build a little game around it, a coin toss, or a race to see who can clean the kitchen the fastest, and then let that person get the first massage?

Spas and beauty supply stores are filled with massage oils they'd love to sell you, but around my thrifty house we make our own. Impressed? Don't be. All you need is a bottle of almond kernel oil and a small bottle of your favorite essential oil. Pick them both up in a health food store. Add thirty drops of essential oil to the almond oil, shake, and you now have your own private label massage oil. Rub away!

Keep It Clean

68

Face it, girls, it is hard to get in the mood for romance when your world is looking sloppy. Dirty clothes on the floor, dishes you *know* you have to wash, and a floor that hasn't seen a vacuum in a week or more—this is not a scenario that will let you relax and appreciate your partner's attentions, is it?

My house is far from pristine on a regular basis, but there is one room that is picked up at all times: the master bedroom. That's right; I make it my one and only house-cleaning priority! Despite the chaos in other rooms of the house, our bedroom is always neat, sweet-smelling, and calm in its clutter-free appearance. No stacks of unopened mail, no piles of old record albums or outdated stereo equipment (although there used to be until I put my foot down!), or extra pieces of furniture. All I need is one room in which I can relax, feel unencumbered by the thought of what else needs to be done, and focus on my love life.

Not up to the task of clearing the clutter out of your bedroom? You can always hire a professional to do the dirty deed for you. Check out the Web site of the National Association of Professional Organizers (www.napo.net) to find one in your area.

Act Like a Mistress

True confession time—I was a mistress once. It was not my finest hour as a woman of honor and integrity. What I kept from the experience, though, was a glimpse into how the humdrum daily business of marriage and family can drive anyone—man or woman—to seek a thrill or two elsewhere.

Here is what a mistress provides: Undivided attention and the feeling of being appreciated, because she listens to his ideas and thoughts instead of always talking about herself. A mistress doesn't nag him about the leaky roof, complain about the visit to his parents, or worry about a note from his child's teacher. She also doesn't act as though she has him all figured out—she gives him space to be someone entirely new and different.

I'm not suggesting that anyone is entitled to have an affair. What I am suggesting is that you be well aware of how a constant focus on the ordinary can snuff out romantic feelings. He's tired of always talking about home life, for instance, and I'll bet you are, too. Declare one night a week to be free from talk about money, the kids, work, the house, the in-laws, or whatever it is that you talk about in an ordinary day. Sit down together and discuss what is in the news, a movie you just saw, or a book you just read. Pretend you are a mistress, and ask him to pretend to be a lover. Who knows where it could lead?

Grow a Love Garden

My husband calls it "growing our love" when we work together in the garden. Personally I think he's just trying to put a romantic spin on hard labor. I do find, though, that the more he gardens, the more often I am presented with a bouquet of freshly picked flowers.

Nature in all forms is romantic, and growing a little bit of nature together is a great way to deepen your connection, especially when you can use the fruits of your labor in the bedroom! Grow an herb garden together. Plant a variety of spices that you can later incorporate into your romantic, candlelit dinners, or use to scent a burning fire, or mix into your massage oil. You might also want to investigate which herbs are used in love potions. Hint: Lavender is a well-known relaxant that can help you loosen up after a long, stressful day. Cloves are said to increase blood circulation and are considered a mild aphrodisiac. Ginger root is said to warm you from the inside out. And that's just the beginning!

All-Day Play

Sometimes you just need to play hooky from the world and phone in sick for the day. Pull the covers up over your head and. . .hey, wait! What if you and your love planned to spend the whole day in bed together? Life doesn't get much more delicious than that!

Just think of the supplies you could bring into the bedroom to make it a relaxation headquarters for the day: lots of wonderful food and drink, all of your favorite movies and old television shows (maybe you can finally watch all those shows you TiVoed), lotions and oils, maybe even an adult toy or two.

Now, I'm guessing that there won't really be day-long action under the sheets. Much activity, yes, but there will also be times when you two are just enjoying the pleasure of hanging out together naked, hidden from the world. This could end up being your favorite holiday of the year!

Fresh Friends

Spicing up your life isn't always about sex. What about the fact that you've had the same friends for the past ten years? You love them, of course; they are fun and reliable, but every so often you need to let some new blood into the crowd. New people bring a fresh perspective, a whole new realm of stories and, best of all, brand new jokes. I'm not suggesting that you dump your current friends (unless you've been secretly seeking permission to do that, in which case, go right ahead). What I am suggesting is that you and your guy make a real effort to involve new people in your lives. Making new friends can prove very difficult as an adult, unless you have something in common.

In my own neighborhood a couple sought out others who lived in what they called "mid-century modern" homes and formed an architectural interest group that now meets every few months to discuss what it is like to live in one of these unique homes (and how to fix the leaky roofs that come along with it). These were all total strangers, brought together by a flyer left in their mailboxes. Why not start your own interest group around something you both feel passionate or curious about? Develop a community garden, organize a couples' hiking group or a book group. Put together a wine tasting group that meets every month (and invite me!). The possibilities are endless.

Truffle Hunters

If you've never heard of truffles before, you might want to take an interest and familiarize yourself. I'm not talking about fancy chocolates; I'm talking about expensive mushroom-like things that pigs sniff out in France and Italy. Here is the reason you should eat truffles: They come packed with a hormone called androstenol. That is actually what makes those horny male pigs snuffle around looking for them around the bases of trees: The smell reminds of them of female pigs. In fact, truffles are sometimes described as smelling like sex. Not surprisingly, they can be found in dishes served on Valentine's Day. Just a small shaving of truffles on top of your dish might put you both in the mood.

Buy a small piece of fresh truffle and store it inside an airtight container filled with white rice. After just a few short days you will be able to cook truffle-flavored rice. And then you should serve your truffle rice with thin shavings of the truffle itself, to get your partner (and yourself) in the mood.

European black truffles can sell for almost one hundred dollars an ounce, so it is no wonder that Americans are trying to figure out how to make them grow here. While I'm not suggesting that you launch a new career as a truffle farmer, I do think you should get a whiff of them and add their sexiness to your plate!

Such Sweet Children

74

I've touched on how hard it can be to feel romantic if your house (particularly your bedroom) is messy. It can be equally hard to feel in the mood if your kids are holy terrors around the house or in public. So, old-fashioned and nanny-ish as this advice sounds, invest time in teaching your children etiquette and good manners. In the same way that treating your partner with courtesy and respect—and receiving it from them as well—pays dividends in the romance department, so will having a house filled with sweet and well-behaved children.

If nothing else, establish privacy rules that allow you and your partner to enjoy uninterrupted time alone. This is extremely important! For little ones who may not fully understand, tie a ribbon on your bedroom doorknob when you are sharing a private moment and explain that they should knock before entering.

If you are relaxed and confident that your children will not come barging in the door, you can be freer to enjoy more romantic moments with your loved one.

Watery Wonders

Nothing makes my heart soar like setting off from the shore in my very own little white dinghy, *The Johnny Deep*, which is festooned with pirate stickers and laden with crab traps. I row away from the shore with my husband on board and a smile on my face. Whether you own a boat or not, there are plenty of ways to enjoy the open seas together.

Always wanted to learn how to sail? Sailing schools are happy to teach beginners, and most boat stores can help you find a beginner's course that will suit you. Don't have time for classes? Rent a canoe one sunny afternoon, and enjoy a picnic lunch together (complete with a bottle of champagne!) on the bank of a river.

Here's an idea that requires very little physical exertion (that is, until you get home): Take a romantic sunset dinner cruise on a nearby lake or ocean. Just imagine sitting on deck with a gentle breeze through your hair, enjoying a candlelit meal and a captivating view at the same time. For a moment, you'll forget everything else that was on your mind, breathe a giant sigh of contentment, and appreciate the moment shared with someone you love.

Sweet Surprises

Let me say it again: Much of ordinary life is dull, and dullness breeds all manner of unpleasant things in your life. So keep boredom at bay by trying to create surprises for yourself and your love on a daily basis.

Surprises don't have to be big; even smallish ones will keep you on your toes: Move the furniture around. Next time you go out to eat, have your partner order something unexpected for you while you powder your nose. Go to a movie theatre and buy tickets for whatever's showing next. Serve dessert before the main course for a change. There are plenty of other ways to add a dose of surprise, so get out your pencil and make a list.

Do I need to remind you that surprises in the bedroom are particularly effective? Maybe you suggest eating dinner naked in bed! Relationships need to have some give and take, though—I don't want you to just *give* surprises; I want you to *get* them, too. Let everyone in your life know that you expect the same thought to go into surprises for *you*. Who knows what they might come up with?

Embrace Bad Weather

We are so accustomed to thinking of inclement weather as the enemy to a good day, but what if it was actually a great opportunity for spontaneity and romance? The next time the skies open up and the rain comes pouring down, forego the scowl, the umbrella, and the rain jacket, and take a walk in the rain with your true love. I guarantee you'll arrive home exhilarated, drenched, and in much better spirits. Help each other out of those wet, clingy garments and into a dry bed, and you'll find that rain is not such a bad thing after all. . . .

Tired of being snowed in when you have about a million things to accomplish in town? Put away the to-do list and drag yourself and your loved one outdoors into that winter wonderland. There's nothing like a good old-fashioned snowball fight or sled race to release tension and bring out your playful sides.

A thunderstorm can be the most romantic form of good old-fashioned entertainment; all it takes is the right attitude, a few glasses of wine, and a view of the sky. Spontaneity is the key to keeping your relationship alive. Look for any and all opportunities, even rainy and snowy ones, to seize the moment.

Meaningful Gems

What woman doesn't love jewelry? The best kind of jewelry, it must be said, is not the most expensive but the kind that holds some special, romantic meaning. It can be a wedding band, a promise ring, a necklace he gave you on your first Christmas together, the earrings you wore on your first date—anything that speaks to your love. Make it a point to wear a piece of meaningful jewelry today—preferably something that your loved one gave you as a gift. It may not be your most flattering piece, but it will definitely flatter and touch the heart of your partner when he sees that you're wearing it. If your wedding band is the most important piece you own, shine it up to give it the attention it deserves.

Now I have a ring that symbolizes great love, and it can go on and be passed to other future generations, too.

How can you add romantic meaning to your regular jewelry? Get it engraved with your combined initials or a short quote that speaks a thousand words. If you're not married, buy a set of matching rings to show the strength of your connection. Don't forget to write down the meaning behind your most romantic jewelry so that future generations will understand where it came from, and why.

Write All Along

So much thought and effort goes into designing and choosing your wedding invitation. Wouldn't it be wonderful if you could relive that uniquely romantic time by having stationery modeled after your invitation?

Find a paper specialty store (Paper Source and Papyrus are both terrific choices) that carries similar card or paper stock, and buy in bulk! Use your new purchase to make thank you notes, party invitations, or monogrammed note cards (you'll need to pay extra to have them professionally printed, or you can save money by printing them at home). If you can't find paper that's similar enough, redirect your search to paper in the colors of your wedding bouquet, or have plain white stationery printed using the same font from your invitation. Was it the curly gold lettering that finally drew you to your wedding invitations? Buy a gold ink pen at any craft store, and use your best cursive to emulate the design.

Remember, what you are after here is another way to remind yourself of how wonderful your wedding day was. On those days when you are ticked off and annoyed, my hope is that you will suddenly notice a bit of wedding-inspired piece of stationery lying around, and suddenly your mood will soften. . . .

What He Really Wants

Every so often we need to back off on the self-improvement programs we all push on our partners and just acknowledge and celebrate who they really are: beer drinking men, most of them. Am I right? So instead of toasting each other with champagne, or Prosecco, or a bit of dry sherry, buy the guy some beers and let him indulge in his fancy.

Why not serve him an Indian beer like Flying Horse (he will love the fact that it is served in enormous, oversized cans) for dinner along with a spicy curry dish and some sexy sitar music for the background? Or pick up a few cans of German beer to serve in the summer with a few sausages tossed onto the grill and a hearty potato salad.

On occasion, I serve my husband his favorite beer—Jamaican Red Stripe. We may not have plans (or cash!) to get away anytime soon, but hey, I can put on a Monty Alexander reggae-infused CD, shimmy into my bikini, and bring out the Red Stripe and Jamaican jerk chicken as often as he wants for an instant vacation.

He'll be grateful when you consider his manly needs and will be willing to express that appreciation later on. . . .

Sweet Treats

Ready for a bit of naughtiness? Here you go: Ever thought about the shape of a donut? A perfect little bundle of goodness that can be slipped right over the top of your partner's—use whatever word you want to here! Wouldn't that be a fun way to start the morning, with a stack of Krispy Kremes and two willing bodies? Yours is the other one, of course, because donuts can be perched on various parts of your willing body, too, ready to be nibbled off the various parts. Be prepared for the stickiness; part of the fun will be showering together afterward.

Food and sex is a fun combination. Tasty treats like chocolate syrup, whipped cream, and even honey are even better when served over exposed body parts. Let your imagination run wild about where you can put the food, and how you can eat it, sip it, or lap it up off each other's body.

Want to make two perky cupcakes for your man on his birthday? Simply squirt a little tuft of whipped cream on each breast and top off with a bright, red cherry. Imagine his thrill when you come out of the kitchen in nothing but a bikini bottom singing the birthday song and wearing his dessert! Totally unlike you? All the better.

Foot Fetish

82

What could be more pleasurable than a foot massage? A full body massage is a delight, of course, but a foot massage can be a spur-of-the-moment treat for either one of you. Just lean over and grab a foot and plop it into your lap. You can do it on the couch, in bed, or any time an unsuspecting foot is nearby and you feel the urge to stroke. But please don't do it while he is driving!

Foot massage can easily be done without massage oils or lotion. Just use firm pressure on the pads of the feet and instep for a bit of acupressure to relieve stress and help eliminate toxins from the body.

Will he then realize that it is your turn for a bit of sexy foot pleasure? He will get the hint if you plop your feet into his lap! If you're too ticklish for a foot massage, suggest that he paint your toenails for you. He may paint outside the lines a little from lack of practice, but you'll feel so special and pampered that you won't even care!

Bejeweled from the Back

Instead of attracting attention to your chest with a necklace and drawing men's eyes downward (Why do you think women started to wear necklaces of that length? It is no accident, dears), why not attract attention to your bare back? The next time you wear a dress with a low-cut back, let a long necklace hang down between your shoulder blades. It should look like a choker from the front. I do this all the time with a long strand of pearls and find it *very* effective! You'll be like the pied piper to men, but the women in the room will be shooting jealous looks your way.

Imagine how sexy you'll feel with the glossy pearls or slippery beads sliding across your bare back and shoulders as you walk. Just the thing to get you in the mood for a more private showing of your jewelry later that evening.

If your bottom is your all-time best feature, try pinning a sparkly brooch to the back of the dress instead. Position it near the base of your spine. Men's eyes will be drawn to your rear end over and over again. Just be warned: Don't try either of these tricks unless you can handle all the attention!

Sexy Accessory

84

I spend a lot of time and energy trying to look like a sophisticated woman of the world who has it all under control. So naturally I want my clothing to put forward this same image (it is so much faster to just buy the look, don't you think?). Here is an easy way to ensure that you'll feel confident, sexy, and well–put together at any event:

Invest in a good evening bag. Yes, that is my simple advice. Spend a little more money than usual on a really swank-looking, black evening bag to wear with simple black pants and a black turtleneck (or that little black dress you wear with your backward pearls). Don't forget your black heels to complete the look. That one simple outfit, and your noticeably chic bag, will take you to any special occasion anytime, anywhere.

Closer to the Action

Picture this—you and your lover are together in a strange city. Instead of hiding behind the safety of a familiar hotel and leaning on the staff for help with your questions, though, you are navigating the new streets with a worn map, negotiating your way through the food markets, and later struggling to light an unfamiliar stove and get your freshly made dinner underway. At night you gaze together out the window at the vista below, toasting the day's brave and adventurous progress.

Fond as I am of hotels (you must go and visit my blog, www.theritzreport.blogspot.com, and see!) the way to adventure frequently lies in taking a more adventurous approach to accommodations than just booking yourself a room at a hotel. Hotels can sometimes stand between you and the sites and the people you want to see. Anything that is closer to what is really happening where you are visiting, beyond the glass doors of a four-star hotel, will give you a whole different level of travel adventure.

Check online for short-term apartment rentals in any city you plan to visit on your vacation, or look for dorm rooms you can stay in during the summer. Visit www.reidsguides.com for lots of info on dorm rooms in Europe. Even more adventurous and devil-may-care is signing up for a house swap. Post your house or apartment on www.digsville.com and see who wants to swap with you!

The Romance Room

Does your house look the same from room to room? All similar colors and artwork on the walls, the carpet never varying? It can be tough to try new things in your life when the landscape never changes. Why not add excitement and romance to your everyday life by completely changing the décor in just one room? Have one room that has such a different flavor that it makes you feel like a whole different person (and perhaps act in a whole different way) upon entering it.

If your house is upbeat and modern, set aside one room to create an air of mystery and intrigue. Paint it a deep, dark color, drape the walls with lush velvet, hang posters from old noir films, and light a bit of incense to add a smoky atmosphere. If you want to, make up a story about who lived in this room and why it is decorated this way. *My great aunt Liddy was an undercover spy, and she picked up these little trinkets on her overseas jaunts. She vanished on a mission some years ago, and we keep the room just so in case she ever does turn up again.*

You'll be glad to have a place where you can stretch your imagination and let your emotions run free.

Fifty Ways to Please Your Lover

Sit down with your lover in a park or a coffee shop and create a list of fifty ways you'd like to be pleased. Why a public place? Just like when you wrote your erotic story in public, you can experience the tingling excitement of getting away with something naughty.

Writing down your deepest, most secret desires helps you to "say" them without having to withstand the discomfort of vocalizing them. Imagine how powerful you will feel when you get his list! What an amazing glimpse into his mind, body, and emotions. Gee, I sure hope he hasn't written the same thing over and over fifty times. . . .

Is fifty too daunting a number? Not all of us can think of fifty different ways we'd like to be pleased, unless you start to include ideas like "take out the garbage." So if fifty is too much, start with ten ways each. Once you've acted on some of your partner's secret desires and he's acted on yours, you'll be perfectly happy to make a longer list.

Hotel Heaven

Yes, I know that just a few minutes ago I was urging you to abandon regular old hotels and embrace the adventure of apartments and house swaps. But if you're going to stay in a hotel, why not stay in one that's beautiful and historic? If you haven't had a chance to create a romance room devoted to mystery and intrigue (#86), a historic hotel can be another great place to play together and stretch your imagination.

Historic hotels that are well worth visiting include the Hotel Del Coronado in San Diego, California, and an amazing hotel built by the Canadian Pacific Railway called The Empress in Victoria, B.C. There are also many old, beautiful homes in New England that have been converted into bed and breakfast lodging. So whenever you are planning a trip, check out the oldest hotel in town—chances are it is also the most interesting. And it makes a perfect rendezvous spot for you and your "secret" lover, or so you imagine.

If you can't afford the room rate at a historic hotel, don't despair. Instead, make a point to meet there for tea or to have a drink in the bar so you can still send yourself to another time and place. Live the romance, and let your imagination run free!

Flicker of Light

What could be more flattering to a woman's complexion than the soft glow of candlelight? Gazing at you across the gently illuminated dinner table, your love will undoubtedly feel more amorous and willing to do your bidding. So why not dine by candlelight *every* night?

With just the strike of a match and the change of atmosphere that ensues, an ordinary dinner can become a slightly more formal and romantic occasion. Make it a plan to dine by candlelight as often as possible. A small investment in a few dozen tapered candles will pay big romantic dividends when your loved one responds to the change. You may both find that you sit up a little straighter and behave a tad more courtly when a more elegant scene is set. Don't worry, the food doesn't have to be fancy and the wine doesn't have to be grand; this small touch goes a long way.

Housewife Fantasy for Two

Every woman has heard the old rumor that magical things happen when you press your body up against the washing machine during the spin cycle. . . . It's probably true, but I've never tried it myself, since it has kind of a lonely, pathetic housewife feel to it. But what if you were to try it with your loved one? Instead of a lonely pathetic housewife, you could be an imaginative and inventive sex partner! A much better image, don't you think? So the next time you two are alone in the house, get a load of clothes going, and tell him what's on your mind. He might even help you gather up the clothes from the floor if you tell him in advance what your plan is!

Fill up the washing machine, press "start," and climb on top. Just you, my dear; I doubt your machine could support two! Once it really starts thumping (maybe you should toss in some tennis shoes that need cleaning?) and vibrating, you can lean back and feel the chores get done while you enjoy some undivided attention. A nice way to spend the afternoon, I'd say.

From Bedroom to Boudoir

Just like the same old lovemaking position can get old after a while, so can the way your bedroom looks! An easy way to spice up your romantic life is to redo the bedroom for a whole new look and feel. Here's the plan: Wait until he goes away for a few days so you can surprise him with all the changes. (I don't recommend doing it this way if you're tight on money. Your plan could backfire if he comes home to find out you've dropped too much dough on new bedspreads, sheets, drapes, and furniture.)

The first thing to do is get all work papers out of the bedroom. Next, visualize a décor that's completely opposite to what you have now. If you're starting with a room that's modern and hard-edged, switch to a soft and cozy nesting spot. If your room is bright and stark, go for dark and mysterious. You don't need to completely redecorate to get a new look. A few new pillows, a small throw rug, and a softer light bulb can work wonders.

Does that sound like too much work? A quicker way to set a romantic tone in the bedroom is to add fresh flowers. Something with a strong scent, like magnolias or lavender, is best as it will charge the air with its romance. Put the flowers in a pretty vase on your nightstand, turn the lights down and the music up, and you have an instant boudoir.

Unplugged

Now that your bedroom has been overhauled for romance, why not do one last small thing. . .unplug the television and cart it out the door. Yes, shocking as it sounds, I firmly believe that the bedroom is no place for a television. Declare your own private relaxing area to be a television-free zone.

Even when both sets of eyes are looking at the same screen, it just isn't romantic—especially when they're glued to the news, a reality show, or one of those creepy investigative shows. Is a forensic thriller really going to get you and your partner into a soft and loving mood? Not likely.

Concentrate instead on spinning a cozy web of romance in the bedroom. Focus on each other and on keeping the mood in the bedroom peaceful and calm. Hint: To ensure that the bedroom is a retreat from all modern nuisances, you may want to extend the technology ban to include cell phones, Blackberries, pagers, and the like.

Have a
Don't Day

Looking for an interesting way to spend a day? Why not declare it a "don't day"? Give yourself the challenge of doing things in a completely different way than usual. Make it a day that you *don't* do anything ordinary.

What are some examples? Don't drive; walk instead. Don't buy anything—not a cup of coffee, not a sandwich for lunch, not even a newspaper. Take one day and don't spend a dime. Don't use the phone! Okay, maybe you could avoid using your cell phone one day, and then all regular phones the next.

Involve your partner by writing down "don't" commands together on separate slips of paper, and then drawing one from a hat. Maybe one of you will pull out a slip that says, "Don't go to work." The other might pull out a slip that says, "Don't laugh," and he will have to try to go the whole day without laughing (which of course will make him laugh harder than usual)! Make sure your "don'ts" are fun and unusual enough to really make you struggle to do something differently.

Or you can try this variation—Have a "do" day where you and your partner must perform *any* sexual request! The more daring one of you gets, the more you'll encourage the other to do the same.

Develop Your Taste

The world does not need another wine connoisseur. We have all had our fill of folks who drone on about the fine points of one wine region or another, or trumpet on about the superiority of one particular type of wine over everything else. Hush up and drink, I say.

You could, however, go out and acquire another kind of expertise. Why not become a connoisseur of sherry instead of wine? Sherry (a fortified wine) has a far more interesting history than plain old wine; one that involves a long, well-known sea voyage to America.

The other nice thing about sherry is that it goes so darn well with dessert—especially if it's a dessert that includes chocolate, coffee, mocha, cinnamon, or molasses. Thus it's the perfect excuse to linger over a dessert tray. You can also get started on your sherry before dinner with a tray of thinly sliced ham, imported prosciutto, nuts, and cheeses like aged blue or brie. Either way, drinking sherry can be a far more interesting and affordable habit than becoming an ordinary wine guru, because there is nothing ordinary about you, right? I didn't think so! Go straight to www.madaboutsherry.com and start learning.

Silken Slips

If you have joined me in a vow to wear more silk, what better place to start than *under* your clothes? That's right, with a silk slip! They're baaack.

Wherever did they go and why? Did we all just rebel at having to wear so much under our clothing? Somewhere along the line, slips developed an old-fashioned and stodgy reputation; they became that thing your grandmother (or heck, great-grandmother) nagged you about putting on before you left the house on a date. The good news is: We can now re-embrace the idea of a silk slip as a very sexy accessory. The smooth feel of it against bare skin justifies its rightful return to popularity.

Spend an afternoon wafting from store to store in search of the perfect silk slip. Don't buy the first one you find; stretch out this sweetly satisfying shopping adventure. Once you find your perfect silk slip, you'll see how wearing it can change the way you feel about an ordinary dress. The outside world will see a well-behaved and properly dressed woman, but you and your lover will know that something sexy is hiding underneath.

Love is in the Air

96

How do you make your cozy, late-evening fire even more romantic and inviting? What if it also smelled good? Then you could both fall under the seductive spell of not just the flickering flames but its soothing aroma as well.

To make a scented fire, go out and buy pine, cedar, or mesquite logs to add to your regular logs. If you love the scent of lavender, toss a handful of dried lavender into the fire to release its heady aroma. Dried rosemary can also do the trick: Simply tuck it under the logs and enjoy the way it perfumes the air with romance.

Citrus lovers may want to try the following: Keep your orange and lemon rinds, and dry them out slowly in a low oven (if you let them air dry on their own, chances are they will mold). Once dry, add them to your fire, and wait for the air to become ripe with the smell of citrus. Breathe in deeply, smile at your love, and let the romantic sensations wash over you!

Hot, Hot Chocolate

Many are aware that chocolate benefits their taste buds, but they may not realize the benefit it can bring to their love lives. The Aztecs believed that chocolate fueled the sexual appetite. As a result ordinary folks were prohibited from drinking hot chocolate—only royalty could enjoy the privilege. Later when the Spanish were mounting a conquest of Mexico, they put a ban on chocolate as a way to keep the population from growing!

Whether it's a bar of pure chocolate, a piece of moist chocolate cake, or a cup of milky hot cocoa, the mysterious powers of this time-honored food are yours to harness. Don't shy away from dark chocolate, either—it has recently been determined to have super-strong, heart-healthy properties. So why not inspire romance and enjoy health benefits at the same time? Fill a tray with bite-sized pieces of dark chocolate, and set it on your bedroom nightstand. It's the perfect appetizer to get things rolling. Here's another way to work chocolate into your love life: Buy a chocolate body tattoo kit and enjoy a night of painting the tattoos on and licking them off.

In With the New

98

You make a list of resolutions every year, don't you: vows to lose weight, another promise not to splurge on shoes, and a serious attempt to beef up your savings account. Why not make another, quirkier list to follow? Sit down, with or without your partner, and draw up a list of twelve new things you'd like to try this year, starting with this month. Your list might include new places you want to travel, new skills you want to acquire, or new people you want to meet.

My Twelve New Things list for last year included a vow to bake my own bread, improve my pencil drawing skills (remember what you could be drawing in #30?), and visit a new country. It also included nine things I'm too much of a lady to mention here. . . . Perhaps your list will include a vow to try twelve different sexual positions this year or to pursue twelve new romantic ideas from this book.

Make sure the items on your list are personally, romantically, or intellectually adventurous. Novelty is what your brain and your body crave; it produces the feel-good chemical dopamine. So if you achieve all twelve before a year is up, get to work on yet another list to challenge yourself in new and interesting ways.

Story Time

Here is a method of seduction I developed in my earlier years: Smile seductively at your intended target, drop your voice down a register, and say these words: "Tell me a story from when you were a little boy." His heart will melt. His defenses will come down and yes, he will tell you a story from when he was a boy. And then he will tell you another one, and another one, and another one. . . .

Why does this work? Because you're asking him to retrace his steps to a time of fun and innocence that everyone is eager to remember. You are encouraging him to open up and share stories about who he was and is today. You are expressing an interest in what matters most to a man—himself.

Once he has shared a story about himself as a child, you will both feel a little closer. Be sure and open up about your own childhood; don't let him be the only one to reveal personal history. Tell funny stories, sad stories, or silly stories about the things you did as a kid: the time you ran around naked when company was over, the day you learned to ride your bike, your very first pet. . . . Connecting in this way could lead to all manner of outcomes, none of which will be childlike!

Keep Your Nails Short

I confess, one of my pet peeves is women who spend too much time and money on their fingernails. It seems so strange to put all of that effort into a habit that actually prevents you from doing exciting things lest you break a nail! If instead you choose to keep your fingernails basic, clean, and short, what kinds of things would you be free to do? In addition to all the time and money you'd save, you could do the following:

- Give your partner a strong and relaxing massage.
- Put your fingers anywhere you want to on your lover's body.
- Give your partner a gentle head or foot rub.
- Climb rocks together.
- Play Frisbee together on the beach.

Go ahead and leave them long enough to give a sexy bit of scratch when you touch him but not so long that you might poke someone's eye out if you aren't careful. Just remember that short fingernails are the mark of an adventurous woman, one who is ready at a moment's notice to plunge into a new opportunity. Short fingernails are supremely sexy!

The Closer I Get to You

101

Ever seen nostalgic photos of high school couples in the '50s sharing a milk shake with two straws? It seems to hearken back to a more innocent time in a budding relationship when you wanted to be as close as possible.

Regardless of how long it has been since you were in high school (or how long it has been since you were innocent, for that matter!), you can have that closeness the next time you go out with your love.

Here is an adult version of sharing a milk shake in a malt shop: Sit together in a restaurant bar at a small, high table and order a meal to share. My husband and I are both quite fond of juicy, succulent prime rib. Our favorite date is also a frugal one—we go to a local steak house, sit together at one of their high bar tables, and split an order of prime rib. We each have our own glass of bourbon, though—you can't skimp on everything! Not only do we save on money and calories, but when we sit so close that our knees touch under the table, and lean in towards each other to eat off the same plate, we get to enjoy that malt shop feeling of closeness in a far more adult setting. Try it the next time you go out, and see if it doesn't send you back!

A Whole New Game

Tired of playing the same old games? I'm not talking about the ones you play early on in a relationship to keep each other interested, but the ones you play when you've been in a relationship too long: Parcheesi, Scrabble, Dominoes, and (gasp) playing cards. If boredom has already led you in this direction, don't worry. There's an easy adjustment you can make to spice things up more than ever!

You can easily turn any board game or card game into a naughty, sex game by incorporating just a little bit of nudity. Forget strip poker; that is far too common, don't you think? Maybe you could play naked Twister! That would be quite a sight to see!

Transform a children's game like Go Fish, Sorry, and Trivial Pursuit into a bedroom game with the simple addition of the "loser strips slowly" rule. Take any ordinary competition and turn it into a voyeuristic celebration of your lover's body. Hate it when he watches sports all weekend? Why not suggest that you root for opposite teams and strip every time the other team makes a point? Suddenly football will get a lot more interesting. . . .

A Head Start
on Romance

Is there anything more relaxing and sensuous than having someone massage your scalp and stroke your hair? I go to the hairdresser far more often than I should just for the pure indulgence of lying back and having someone wash my hair. All it takes is a little reciprocal head massage and hair washing to bring this luxurious and sensual feeling into your relationship.

Start by suggesting your partner lie back with his head on your lap. Place a towel down first to protect your clothes from oils, and then begin stroking, lightly scratching, and massaging his head with just a drop or two of scented massage oil on your hands. Imagine how relaxed and receptive your partner will be once this phase is complete. When he's putty in your hands, lead him to the shower, turn on the water, and finish the job with a thorough hair and body wash.

And when is it your turn? That very same night, I hope! You, too, deserve a relaxing and sensual head and scalp massage, and of course you want him to wash your hair. On those nights when neither of you has time for a full-out massage, perhaps you could request a gentle hair brushing. Sit back and relax as he gently runs a brush through your lustrous locks. You'll feel loved, pampered, and relaxed all at once.

In Formal Attire

All men look good in a tuxedo: so crisp and elegant in black and white; so slim in a snug cummerbund; so James Bond, sophisticated and in control.

But not all men will wear a tuxedo willingly, my own husband included. So let me share the secret of getting your man to dress up willingly. . . . Here's the plan. Step one: Get him a tuxedo. Step two: A few weeks before the event in question, ask him to put it on. Tell him he can be naked except for the jacket and tie, and then use all of your womanly skills to make that a very, very memorable evening for him. And step three? Who needs it? Trust me, in the future he will put on a tuxedo willingly for major events in anticipation of taking it off afterward!

Break the Rules

When was the last time you broke a rule and did something that you *knew* you weren't supposed to do? I hope it wasn't a *major* rule you were breaking, but didn't it feel good? Imagine how it would feel if, as a couple, you broke a smallish rule or two every now and then. . . . You have my permission to go ahead and be naughty together! Remember how that dopamine chemical is produced by novel events, by trying new things? Breaking a tiny rule will give you a tiny jolt of dopamine to jazz things up.

Now I don't imagine you both becoming a latter-day Bonnie and Clyde story terrorizing the countryside, but maybe you'll park your car somewhere you shouldn't and take a short walk. Don't endanger yourselves or others; please obey signs that indicate a real danger. But go ahead and step on the grass or pick a forbidden flower every now and again.

My husband, Peter, and I smoke cigars together—heaven forbid if our parents knew! And to add a bit of extra thrill, we smoke *Cuban* cigars whenever we can get our hands on them! Naughty indeed.

Surprise Message

Sometimes you want to send a sweet or racy message to your loved one, but you don't want anyone else to read it. What to do? If you put it in his lunch bag or briefcase like all those other romance books suggest, someone else might be standing next to him as he discovers it, and an embarrassing situation could arise!

Try this idea instead: Use a bright colored lipstick to write a suggestive or romantic message on the bathroom mirror where he'll be sure to see it. (Just make sure that he is the only person who will be using that bathroom anytime soon, or confine your creative remarks to the master bathroom.) Imagine the lift it will give him to look up while brushing his teeth in the morning and see "I love you" written there, just for him. Or to come home at the end of a long day, when you're already fast asleep, and see "I'm naked and waiting under the covers" written in hot pink lipstick. You may waste a little lipstick in the deal, but his reaction will be worth it.

Walk in Nora Roberts' Shoes

Nora Roberts is one of the most famous romance authors of our time. Ever read one of her best sellers? If you are a fan—or even if you are just planning to write a romance novel yourself—why not get inspiration from renting one of her beach cottages? She and her husband, Bruce Wilder, own three small cottages that are available for weekly rental on Hatteras Island, North Carolina.

Imagine: You could stay in one of the very houses and gaze out at the very scenery that inspires Nora Roberts to produce so much of her work! You could walk the same floors, lie on the same bed, and look out the same windows as a woman who spends her waking hours dreaming up romantic scenarios and dialog for the rest of us to swoon over. Who knows what you might be inspired to do? If you don't begin writing your own romantic work (this would be a great place to compose your erotic novel), you and your love might choose to spend the weekend creating enough action to fuel a dozen romance novels.

To find her houses, log onto www.hatterasvacations.com and click on "cottage search." Roberts and her husband own the ocean-view cottages named "Nora," "Wilder View," and "Royal-T."

It's a
Wrap!

I'll bet you have a favorite romance movie, one that makes you sigh and smile every time you think of it. Wish you could step inside the film and live the romance for a day? All you have to do is take some element of that film and incorporate it into your own life. If it's *Sleepless in Seattle* that gets you in the mood, why not meet your partner at the tallest building in town for a romantic get-together? If it's *Dirty Dancing*, ask your loved one to take a dance class with you or teach you something he knows really well (imagine his hands on your hips as you practice your golf swing.

What if every time you walked through your bedroom or opened your closet door, you caught sight of a small relic from that movie? Check out www.itsawraphollywood.com, where they auction off props, costumes, and collectibles from movies and television shows. Once there, you could also purchase sexy clothing worn by Hollywood's hottest actress. What man wouldn't have a special thrill reaching out to touch a dress worn by Angelina Jolie?

Turnabout is fair play, of course, so you could also buy something worn by your favorite actor and dress your husband in that! I could have bought Johnny Depp's shirt from the movie *Sleepy Hollow* on the Web site www.propstore.com if I had moved a little faster.

Not-So-Secret Gardens

While your own small, backyard garden is probably very sweet and pretty, giant public gardens are where romance truly flourishes. Seek out public gardens with acres and acres of flowers both indoors and out, one you can get lost in. Experience the romance of wandering for hours on winding dirt paths through a sea of color, admiring one gorgeous bit of nature before quickly becoming captivated with the next.

Put on a long flowing skirt (I know you bought one after reading #33) and wander through the orchid show at the New York Botanical Garden in the Bronx. They hold it every year and bill it as "America's premier exhibition and sale of orchids." Orchids are also very much in display across the country in San Francisco's Conservatory of Flowers. You will be inspired by the sight of several hundred types of orchids found inside this sparkling crystal palace, the oldest conservatory in the Western Hemisphere. Walk the aisles reciting poetry quietly to yourself. Breathe in the romance all around you as you walk hand in hand with your love in the midst of such beauty. Be sure to bring along a picnic lunch for afterward, ando pack a bottle of sparkling Prosecco to toast nature's wonders.

The Daring Traveler

Do you ever find yourself traveling alone on business, shut up in the evenings in a lonely hotel room with only CNN as a companion? No more! Choose a life of adventure instead! Get up off the bed, ask the hotel staff where the locals go, and head on out the door. Women of the world get out and dine alone if they have to when traveling; they don't stay shut up in their bland hotel rooms with a wilted room service salad. You've eaten enough of those, haven't you?

Never miss an opportunity to get to know another city and its people. Talk to the locals any chance you get. I have my own little ritual when traveling: I ask the front desk where I can find a great piece of pie. Pie gets folks talking; they smile and happily offer up their favorite places. Once I've got my hot tip about the town's best pie joint, I head straight there and sit at the counter (because you know all good pie places are diners). I order the pie, and chat up the waitress about her life. Nine times out of ten it is the start of a fun and interesting conversation with someone I've never met in a place I'll never visit again.

So go out into that strange town. Smile and make eye contact. I'm not suggesting you have some little fling on the road, only that you are adventurous enough to break out of your shell and experience new things.

Use Your Senses

Close your eyes, focus, and tune into the sounds, smells, and sensations that surround you. Are there birds chirping outside your window? Can you smell newly mown grass? Do you feel a soft blanket against your skin? It's important to pay attention to what your other senses reveal to you when you deprive yourself of sight.

Sensuous women are able to enjoy even the smallest aspects of life by focusing on their senses. Becoming more aware of what your senses are telling you translates into your ability to enjoy romance and work yourself into the mood anywhere, anytime.

Don't believe me? Think about it this way—Now that the smell of curry or Turkish food seems romantic (you remember that night in the pillows at the restaurant, don't you?), you may suddenly find yourself aroused in the spice aisle at the grocery store! Now that the feel of cool pearls against your skin has a sexual meaning to you, watch out!

Your heightened senses can take you to higher levels of pleasure, so it's in your best interest to use them anytime, anywhere. Just lie back, close your eyes, and let go. . . .

Liquid Gold

112

Invite some friends over to enjoy some appetizers or dessert served with a very, very expensive bottle of wine. I'm not suggesting that you front the cost yourself—because stress from overspending can ruin any relationship. Instead, why not choose a wine that none of you would be able to buy and enjoy on your own and then split the cost? This will be your chance to try some of the remarkable wines on the market for a fraction of the cost.

I've always wanted to drink the famed dessert wines from Chateau D'Yquem, but the $150 price tag is way out of my reach. By making a selection of desserts that would work well with it—citrusy tarts—and then inviting over a few other wine lovers to help split the cost, I was able to enjoy the experience for closer to $25.

Pooling your money to buy an adventurous wine is a wonderful basis for an evening shared with several couples. See, romance on a budget doesn't have to be dull!

Warm It Up

Much as you and your partner love to be massaged, you may grow tired of using the same greasy oils. What to do? Try some warm lotion instead. The heat will help to loosen up your muscles and won't shock your skin as cool lotion would.

To take the chill off any lotion, place the tube or container in a small saucepan of hot water and leave it there for a few minutes to heat up. There are now actual machines that will heat your lotion up for you—Conair makes a heated lotion dispenser that would be perfect on your nightstand.

For something a little new and different, run down to the drugstore and look for warming lubricant (the KY Jelly folks have one) or condoms with warming action. Warm is in big time, baby: The folks at www.edenfantasys.com will sell you what they call "motion lotion," which is a flavored lotion that heats up when applied. Just the way to take the chill off a cold winter's night!

Night
Pearls

There are several ways to feel sexy with pearls (as you've seen in #13 and #83). Another way is to give them a double life: sophisticated by day, naughty by night.

Remember those iconic photos of Jackie Kennedy in her three-strand pearl choker? She looked so classy, so demure. Worn during the day with a suit, a pearl choker like Jackie O's indicates a woman of breeding and impeccable manners. But that same piece of jewelry can take on a whole other look and feel at night when worn with a low-cut dress. Give it a try and experience it for yourself.

Wear a pearl choker to the office with a button-up shirt or a plain, tailored suit. Spend your professional day imagining how you'll transform into your nighttime identity. Later that evening, make it a point to appear before your loved one in nothing but the choker and your lingerie, or absolutely nothing at all but your pearls. So much for demure; you'll look downright naughty!

Who says diamonds are a girl's best friend? I vote for pearls!

Acts of Love

Your mother told you this a hundred times growing up—actions speak much louder than words. She was probably talking about your frequent promises to clean up your room, but it also applies to romantic relationships. What matters most in a long-term relationship is not what partners say but what they do.

The way you both act—day in and day out, sun up to sun down, and every time in between—is what ultimately will make yours a romantic and loving relationship. You can't flip through this little book and suggest an idea to bump up the action on a Friday night if on Thursday you took out your bad day at work on him. And he can't expect you to care about his Fifty Ways to Please Your Lover list (#87) if he just blew off your anniversary to go golfing. Our bodies don't work that way: We don't get hot for people who tick us off.

So remember, you can't just talk about love and romance, and you can't just swap declarations of undying love and devotion without also practicing showing that love in small ways every chance you get. The smallest gestures, from a warm smile across the room to the arrival of a cup of coffee and a newspaper in bed, will all add up to the life of romance, spice, and adventure you both deserve.

The Big Squeeze

Looking for a way to pass the time as you wait for the light to turn green; for your turn at the check-out line; or for the Muzak to end and a real voice to come on the line? You could be squeezing and releasing the most private muscles your body has—the muscles inside your vagina. It might not sound appealing at first, but the stronger and tighter those muscles are, the easier it is to have an orgasm (or two or three) and the more intensely you will feel it (or them). Sound like a workout you could benefit from? It gets even better: Your lover may also benefit from better orgasms once you develop that stronger "gripping" action.

The exercises are called Kegels and were invented to help women tighten things up after having babies. How often should you do them? Start with just a few and work up to doing slow sets of thirty. Hold the muscle for ten seconds before releasing. Use the same ones you would use to stop urinating midstream. You could be sitting in a parent/teacher meeting at school, Kegel-ing away while listening to a detailed description of the new curriculum. Aren't you the wicked one, working on your sex life in a public setting.

Delicious Interludes

Having breakfast in bed is a fine habit that you should indulge in often. It's so pleasant to begin the day with a cup of coffee, a crisp newspaper, and a few precious, relaxed moments before you both start into your busy routine. Why not end your day the same way?

Put that breakfast tray to use at night for a change! After the rest of the household is quietly tucked in and (hopefully) asleep, load up your breakfast tray with a few favorite dessert goodies. Cups of decaf coffee or tea, fresh strawberries, a dollop of dessert sauce, gooey puddings, and ice cream are some delectable options. Try to stay away from the crumbly cakes and cookies that might leave crumbs in your bed—no one wants to sleep on the remnants of a late-night cookie feast.

Use your nighttime snack-in-bed moment to share stories of your day, make quiet plans for tomorrow, and laugh at what went wrong at the office. This quiet closeness will help you ease into a restful sleep, or better yet, a very loving mood. Who knows where that dessert sauce could end up?

Love
Symbols

I once knew a couple who passed a small wooden heart back and forth for years as a message of love to each other. She would reach her hand into her jacket one day for change and find the wooden heart that her husband had hidden there. Then it was her turn to hide it somewhere so he would stumble across it unexpectedly. It was a sweet game they created where quiet, out-of-the-blue statements of love would undoubtedly lead to a fruitful evening.

What if you took this a bit further? Choose a secret symbol that you and your loved one could use to indicate an interest in sex. I'm not talking about leaving a banana on his pillow, but something subtle like draping your favorite silk nightgown across the bed. If he notices it there in the morning, he'll have all day to think about you and the night ahead. Perhaps he would place a flower on your pillow to let you know he was thinking of you and looking forward to the end of the day. Imagine the fun you'll have deciding on a secret signal; one that only the two of you know about. That way you can use it in public without anyone else suspecting your intent.

Are we having steak tonight, dear? could be a code phrase with a meaning only you understand. There's nothing like a sexy secret to bind two people together.

Distant Dream

Satisfying as it is to finish any kind of project on your own, it is also highly satisfying to work side by side with your loved one for years on end to achieve a big project together. Refinish an old wooden boat; restore an old house together; work on some kind of long-term, large-scale project (other than raising children) that will take years and years to complete.

Choose something that allows you both to look to the future and imagine yourselves enjoying the fruits of your labor together—driving along a coastal highway in your newly restored roadster, sailing together to Hawaii in the boat you made, drinking wine on the stone patio you carved out of a rocky hillside. Of course there may be a few fights and some ups and downs along the way, but that's all part of the journey. So keep your eye on the long-term goal of completion and closeness.

Stop Thinking So Much

Your mother wanted you to be practical, but I'm here to tell you gently that practicality seldom leads to adventure and romance. Why not be impractical for a change? Give your love life a quick boost by checking your intellect at the door. Even if it's just for a day or an evening or a moment, you'll be invigorated by the experience.

I'm not talking about throwing away the leftovers after dinner (though this might help get you in the right mindset); I'm talking about buying expensive silk sheets for the bed, even if they aren't machine washable. I'm suggesting that in your haste to get each other's clothes off, it's okay to leave the candles lit regardless of whether some wax could drip onto the nightstand. Leave the fireplace burning all night so you can sleep in front of it—forget about the gas bill for once. Be late for work so you can enjoy some playtime with your loved one. Jump into the lake, even though your hairdo might get ruined. If you can manage to hush the no-nonsense voices inside your head (especially your mother's), you'll be free to experience the spontaneity that is so crucial to romance.

Pour the Champagne

Remember #8, new uses for old champagne? Well, here is a way to make sure that you have some leftover champagne in the house at all times: Include it in your sex life! With any luck, you'll be less than halfway through the bottle before you forget all about finishing it.

Bring the bottle and two glasses into the bedroom for a little experimentation. Take a small sip, hold the bubbly liquid in your mouth, and then lean over and apply your mouth to your partner's eager body. Try not to spill. Wait until you see the reaction you get when the cold and bubbly liquid inside your warm mouth reaches its intended target! You have now learned a whole new way to enjoy champagne.

What happens when it's your turn? Encourage your partner to pour a tiny bit of icy cold bubbly over your belly button or the small of your back, and then slowly lap it off.

Sound a teensy bit too wild? For the shy and traditional, just keep a chilled bottle and glasses on the nightstand. Maybe after a few glasses, you'll feel free enough to try one of these suggestions, or think of a new use on your own. Please: If you think of something new, e-mail it my way!

The Simple Truth

Live simply, love simply. It may sound trite, but I mean to make
a serious point here—that so much of our modern day, high-
maintenance lifestyle intrudes on our ability to relax and enjoy
what is actually happening in our lives. Instead of spending
quiet time with a loved one, we are way too busy working hard
to pay for all of the things that we *must* have.

So simplify, already. Refocus your life on your loved ones,
your friends, even your garden—anything but the constant pursuit of expensive stuff that requires you to work long and hard.
Get rid of everything that is cluttering up your life, from expensive toys and gadgets to the overwhelming commitments you
have made that prevent you from spending time at home. My
guess is that you've joined too many committees, make too
many trips to the mall, and have many things that need to be
removed from your life before you can sit next to your love and
share a relaxed laugh and not worry about where you need to be
and what you need to be doing. Keep it simple, and then enjoy
the peace that comes from it.

Scented Locks

Perfumed hair has an antiquated sound to it; it's the sort of thing women did centuries ago to disguise the fact that they hadn't bathed or washed their hair in a year or two. Not all women who perfumed their hair lived so long ago, though. Jackie Kennedy was known to sprinkle cologne on her hairbrush at night before she brushed her fifty to one hundred strokes. An old-fashioned technique, yes, but it clearly helped her win the hearts of more than one man!

How can you get a bit of scent into your lustrous locks? Spritz your hairbrush with a tiny bit of cologne before brushing and that should do the trick. Don't do it every single time you use the hairbrush, though. You are aiming for a subtle effect here; something that, when you pass by, makes a man lift his head and think, *What was that nice smell?*

To get this effect anytime you need it, tear a few perfume sample pages from your favorite magazine and store them in your purse. Whenever you need a sexy lift, just pull out a sample, open the flap, and rub the perfume gently over your hair. Instant elegance.

Wear Less Lingerie

Truth be told, I wanted to call this book *Wear Less Lingerie*. Why would I ever encourage women to wear *less* lingerie in a book about leading a sexy and romantic life?

Well my dears, I think you now know that a good love life might include a black lace bra and matching panties, but it doesn't depend on them. When you have unlimited access to the greatest sex toy ever invented—your juicy imagination—you don't need anything else.

Am I asking you to give up your pretty underclothes? Heavens, no. Wear whatever you enjoy the most: It could be the long flowing skirt you bought to conjure up an earlier time, or the seemingly demure strand of pearls that takes on another life at night. But whatever you wear, remember that it's just an accessory to a sexy and inventive "anything goes" attitude.

Look Out for Ghosts

Need an excuse to hold your lover's hand and snuggle up close? Why not book a weekend at one of the many hotels that claim to be haunted? Sometimes the ghost is lovelorn—wandering the halls moaning in search of a lost love. Sometimes the ghost is simply a devoted employee—one hotel is haunted by a uniformed bellman, of all things. Do you still have to tip him if he is dead?

Any weekend away in a hotel can be romantic, of course, but purposely staying somewhere with ghosts adds a sense of thrill and adventure. Among the hotels that advertise their otherworldliness are The Queen Mary (a retired cruise ship) in Long Beach, California; the Stanley Hotel (where Stephen King wrote *The Shining*) in Estes Park, Colorado; the hotel Del Coronado in San Diego, California; and the regal Fairmont Banff Springs Hotel, in Alberta, Canada, where that ghostly bellman might help you with your bags.

If a hotel trip isn't in your budget, why not just rent the movie *Ghost* with Demi Moore? It is a spooky, romantic tearjerker that will have you not only holding your lover's hand but sniffling as well.

Erotic
Word Play

Want to send a sexy message to your lover but feeling too shy to write the words down on a page? Here is another, somewhat slyer, way to convey your mood. You get to enjoy making it, and he gets to enjoy doing it. And by "it" I mean an erotic puzzle, of course!

The first step is to decide what you want the puzzle to say— Will it be a naughty suggestion? A sexy promise? An idea for a new rendezvous spot? Or a list of locations where you've enjoyed the most romantic vacations? Once you have your message, pull out a Scrabble board and use the tiles to arrange the words of your message so that some or all of them interlock like a crossword. Transfer that arrangement to paper, using an empty box to represent each letter.

Now start writing clues that will help your partner decipher your puzzle. Little words like *and* and *the* can be hinted at through the names of movies, couples, or song titles. For instance, use "Bonnie _ Clyde," to get him to guess the word *and*.

Once you both get the hang of erotic puzzling, you can do it anywhere, anytime. Forget about tucking a sweet message in your husband's lunch bag—pop in an erotic puzzle instead and see how fast he drives home!

Fit for a Queen (or King)

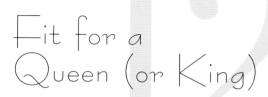

Many years ago I asked my husband, Peter, to work up a list of ideas he thought were romantic. His favorite idea was to sneak into the bedroom and prepare the bed as though you were spending the night in a hotel and the maid had come to get it all ready for you. Here's a great way to create a relaxing and inviting "we're on vacation" mood without any of the expense: While he's occupied, sneak into your bedroom, fluff the pillows, turn down the covers, leave flowers on the nightstand, set a chocolate on each pillow, and lay out a robe and slippers for each of you. Now lead him blindfolded into the bedroom and, once you've truly piqued his curiosity, show off your handiwork. What a great surprise for an otherwise ordinary evening!

For a less budget-conscious treat, you can actually *buy* the bed used by your favorite hotel. Ritz-Carlton Hotels will sell you the special Sealy Posturpedic Plush mattress that they use in their rooms, and the Four Seasons has long made their bedding available to their guests. Many hotels will sell you the high thread count sheets as well, to help you complete the hotel look and feel in your bedroom.

A word to the wise: Just don't present a bill in the morning.

Candle Stacks

A blazing fire in your fireplace is wildly romantic in the fall or winter, but not particularly appealing in the warm summer months. So how can you replicate the romantic, flickering glow without the excess heat? Simply build a stack of candles in your fireplace.

You'll need ten heavy, round candles. They don't all have to be the same color (unless you prefer that look), but they do need to be the same size: I use 3 x 3 pillar candles for my candle stacks.

Place four of the candles in a row inside your nicely cleaned fireplace. Space them out an inch or so apart. Stack another three candles on top of the bottom four, straddling the spaces in between them. Make another row of two candles that straddle the spaces between the lower three. And on top, place the final candle. Now light them all and enjoy the spectacle!

When using your decorative candle stack, check it frequently to make sure that the bottom stack of candles isn't melting too fast to keep the structure secure. Romance doesn't include a small fire on the carpet, so keep an eye on things, please.

Spend Yourself!

129

Over and over I've been telling you not to spend money, but here is what I do want you to spend: yourself. That's right; to fully lead a life of romance, spice, and adventure you need to give yourself over in the process.

What does it mean to *spend* yourself? It means you put yourself out into the world and take chances, try new things, meet new people, and offer your love and ideas and energy to the people around you. It means you share your honest feelings, you open up to reveal your inner thoughts, and you trust that others will do the same with you. If you selfishly hoard the best parts of yourself, you are not living life to its fullest.

> *"Life begets life. Energy begets energy. It is only by spending oneself that one becomes rich."*
> —*Sarah Bernhardt*

I keep that quote in a jeweled frame in my office so that I remember to ask: Have I spent myself lately or am I hoarding myself and my energy, letting it sit on the shelf or be locked away in a vault to grow dusty over time? Don't forget to ask yourself that question every now and then.

Stars in Your Eyes

130

Sometimes nature gives us the most sumptuous displays of all, if we only remember to look at the sky above us. Several times a year there are meteor showers that fill the sky like sparklers, giving us a rare opportunity to see one shooting star after another.

What a sweet way to spend an evening with a lover, lying together on a think blanket rolled out on the grass, watching the sky explode before your very eyes. Yes, of course you should sometimes share meteor showers with your children, as it is a wonderful way to see science on parade, but do save a night or two for yourself.

How do you find out when the showers are likely to appear? The two major showers are Perseid and Leonid, and you can learn more about them online at www.stardate.org/nightsky/meteors/

Wear More Silk!

My deep love of cashmere led me to write a book on pampering called *Wear More Cashmere*. It's no secret that I'm all in favor of any fabric that feels fabulous against my skin, adds a flattering glow to my complexion, and makes me feel like a princess. (Feel like a queen if you must, but I'd rather be a princess— same amount of jewelry, less responsibility.)

It's time to praise the wonders of silk; cool, smooth flowing silk that slides easily across the skin. Fill your life with its sensual allure—provide yourself with silk to sleep in, silk for every day, silk for business meetings, silk to tie up your hair when the wind blows, and silk to tie up your partner when the desire strikes. It may be that a simple silk shift is already hanging in your closet; something you bought on a tropical vacation and have let languish ever since. Don't let it go to waste—slip it on and wear it to bed tonight.

Silk is an attitude, my dears—a sensual and vibrant attitude that will help you move through life demanding romance, adventure, and the biggest helping of spice there ever was! You deserve it all—now go out and get it for yourself!

Acknowledgments

In a book on romance and adventure, I would like to thank all of the many friends—men and women—who have bravely accompanied me on some of my adventures. I'll thank the women first: Sherry, who pushed tirelessly on through the sweaty jungles of Indonesia in an effort to keep up with our handsome hired guide; Cathleen, who is always up for a snowy afternoon on the slopes or a wine-filled evening; Judith and Jane, who are always willing to enroll in a night class or discuss the merits (or failings) of a new book; and my globe-trotting sister Anne, who is frequently embarrassed by what I do but is nevertheless a cheerful supporter.

And as for the men—it may behoove me as a long-married woman to merely wave in grateful but silent acknowledgment to my handsome and interesting but long-since departed former beau. But I can loudly and publicly thank my own partner in romance and adventure, Peter Julian Sander, for his constant attention and apparent appreciation for my offbeat approach to life.

Thanks also to the fabulous staff at Fair Winds Press, who have seen me through so many books. Ellen, Holly, and friends, you are the best.

About the Author

A longtime fan of luxury, silk-savvy Jennifer (known to her friends as "Gin") Sander is the best-selling author of more than a dozen books, including *Wear More Cashmere*, *The Martini Diet*, and *MomSpa*. The busy mother of two boys, she years ago began to make a list of little things she could do to spice up her life, and eventually her ideas grew to 131!

Jennifer and her books have been featured on *The View* with Barbara Walters, *American Journal*, C-Span's *Book TV*, *Fox and Friends*, and *It's a Miracle*. Articles about Jennifer have appeared in *USA Today*, *New York Newsday*, *Cosmopolitan*, the *Boston Globe*, the *Los Angeles Times*, the *Sacramento Bee*, and many other magazines, newspapers, and television shows. A popular public speaker, she lives in Northern California.